'A beautifully touching memoir of a 1980s childhood lived through the prism of sport. It's a book about family, about what it means to be young, about the lessons learned and the bonds forged through a young boy's obsession with football, snooker, hurling, golf, darts and anything else going. Full of heart and equally full of fun, there are chuckles of recognition to be had from every page. If you ever strung a length of washing line across the road to try to replicate the excitement of Wimbledon, if you played street football while imagining John Motson simpering over your every touch, if you trotted around an obstacle course slapping your backside during Dublin Horse Show week, or if you tried to emulate Alex Higgins on a four-foot by two-foot snooker table in the tight confines of a suburban kitchen, then *Boy Wonder* will make you ache with nostalgia for your own childhood. I will treasure it along with my first O'Neill's replica Liverpool kit.'

PAUL HOWARD

'Utterly authentic, Dave Hannigan captures Cork of that era perfectly. He does so with all the style, panache and effectiveness of Jimmy Barry-Murphy with a hurley in his hand. Cork people will get that – indeed, most Irish sports lovers will too.'

MATT COOPER

Acknowledgements

Following the death of my mother in 2015, my brother Tom began the painful process of emptying our family home in Togher. Almost every week, he sent me one more photograph, book or magazine that evoked a thousand memories, nearly all of them warm and wistful. This book, I guess, came from sifting through the memorabilia and paraphernalia of a childhood, each physical object conjuring up different emotions, stirring memories of my parents, Theresa and Denis, my brother, my sisters, Anne (RIP) and Denise, and a house, like most, that overflowed with noise, laughter, chaos and love.

These are the people and places that make you who you are and shape what you become. These are the people who inspired me to tell these stories. I will forever be grateful to my parents, siblings, and all the residents of the Clashduv Road area, Ian O'Leary, Stephen Mehigan, Barry Geoghegan, especially, for the boyhood they gave me.

As per hoary old cliché, there are too many people to thank for bringing this book to fruition but it would be remiss of me not to express my gratitude to Conor Nagle whose enthusiasm, encouragement and support for a rather unorthodox project was infectious. Elsewhere at Gill Books, Sheila Armstrong did a wonderful job nursing the book through the various stages of production and Sine Quinn, bringing her exceptional editing skills to bear, made some serious improvements to the manuscript. The quality of the fantastic design job by Fergus O'Keeffe is evident in your hands today.

Debts of various kinds are owed to many, many people, some of whom have listened to versions of these tales for decades. A by no means conclusive list includes Emmet Barry, PJ Browne, Dave Clarke, Tommy Conlon, Ken Cotter, Paul Howard, Enda McEvoy, Michael Moynihan, Colm O'Callaghan, Gavin O'Connor, Rob O'Driscoll, Mark O'Loughlin, Kadie Pearse, Mark Penney, Fergus Roche, Ger Siggins and Denis Walsh.

For continued professional support I would like to thank Malachy Logan (*Irish Times*), John Dolan and Maurice Gubbins (*Evening Echo*), Ray O'Hanlon and Peter McDermott (*Irish Echo*).

Thirteen years have passed since I first drove through the gates of Suffolk County Community College where I have found a home far from home. My friends and colleagues there, especially those in the social sciences department, have given me friendship and so much more.

My mother-in-law Clare Frost yet again served as a rigorous reader of the first draft and I would like to thank her and her husband George for all they continue to do for my family. My wife Cathy and my sons, Abe, Charlie and Finn tolerated way too many evenings when I sat in front of the laptop with a pair of old, tiny, white soccer boots in my hand, a smile on my face and a faraway look in my eye. Thank you all for your patience. I'm back from Cork now.

For Abe, Charlie and Finn, my darling boys

Prologue

My father grew up on Blarney Street on the northside of Cork city in the 1940s and '50s, a time of harsh economic conditions when children didn't have much. And so, whenever I beseeched him to buy me anything, he always summarily dismissed my plea by declaring, 'When I was your age, I had a hoop!' That was the prelude to an inevitable spiel about how he and his resourceful peers never needed gadgets or toys to amuse themselves.

A hoop, it was eventually explained to me, was a bicycle wheel that had the spokes taken out. He and his friends entertained themselves by rolling these hoops up and down inclines and steps around Blair's Hill and Sunday's Well, steering them with sticks, marvelling at the speeds they could reach. When that was what passed for recreation back in his time, little wonder then that he gave me short shrift every time I wanted something new and shiny.

One day last summer, I stood in my house in suburban Long Island, three thousand miles from where I grew up in Cork, and I heard my three sons declare themselves bored.

'We have nothing to do,' they chorused.

At the time they were sitting in a room that contained every piece of sporting equipment known to man, and a range of electronica that included a PlayStation, a computer, a pair of Kindle Fires and an iPod Touch. To quell my growing anger, I picked up my hurley from the hallway and launched into a soliloquy.

'You see this?' I shouted, brandishing it above my head. 'Where I grew up in Togher, this wasn't just a hurley. This was a sword if we wanted to fence. It was a rifle if we wanted to wage war. It was a paddle if we wanted to go sailing. It was even a cricket bat if wanted to pretend to be English!'

They looked at me derisively. Children of their generation, as assuredly as I was a product of mine, they were unimpressed by my passionate trip down memory lane, unmoved by my attempt to explain how a little imagination can go a long way. My bygone days every bit as irrelevant to them as my father's once were to me.

I walked from the room, defeated, deflated, and under my breath, for the first time in my adult life, I muttered the words, 'When I was your age, I had a hoop.'

In the end, we all become our fathers.

ONE

Dive of My Life

Thirty feet above ground, I picked some flecks of peeling paint from my skin and looked clear across the dressing-room rooftops below me, each one coated in a sprinkling of nuclear green moss. There were cars whizzing by on the Straight Road down to my left. I glanced at them for a blurry second and exhaled. I was seriously out of breath. I had clambered at great speed up three different storeys of the concrete diving board structure, scraping my chest and belly off the sharp edge of each one in order to reach the very top.

The highest level of the diving platform had been placed off-limits that season and the springboard removed. The ladders leading from storey to storey had been taken out as well, to discourage anybody from getting up there to take a chance of going off without something to launch from. Of course, these precautions added a whiff of the illicit to the whole enterprise and made everybody that bit more determined to give it a whirl. I'd watched boys and girls made of sterner stuff make that arduous climb all summer long in search of a sliver of glory. Now it was my turn.

On the other side, I could see poachers in Polaroid sunglasses stalking fish by the gargling white-capped weir of the River Lee. It was too far away for me to make out if any of them were my uncles. In any case, I had other concerns on this particular day than wondering if we'd have ill-gotten salmon, wrapped hastily in a flattened cardboard box, being delivered to our backdoor just in time for tea.

I kept looking to the sides. It made much more sense than bearing straight down. Straight down was a precipitous drop into fifteen feet of uninviting water. A long, long way down.

A breeze blew up. Or it may just have been a shiver mounting my spine now that I realised just how high up the top level actually was. Thirty feet didn't sound like that much until you climbed it. I was suddenly cold, nervous and starting to become the butt of jokes.

'This fella thinks he's a regular Greg Loouugaaaniiisss,' shouted a teenage voice, rolling the name around his tongue, relishing every vowel and consonant.

I didn't need to look down to imagine this wit leaning on the metal fence that ran around the diving pool. I'd often been there myself, throwing insults at wannabe heroes, mocking them as shapers, showing off for any girls within earshot. My own cheeks reddened knowing I was now the centre of attention for the peanut gallery and their chorus of barbs, especially because there was enough supplementary guffawing to suggest more and more people were gathering to see me attempt to make my dive. To stake my claim.

I did not think I was Greg Louganis. I may have desperately wanted to be Greg Louganis although I could do without the snug Speedos he wore. Obviously. I was a soccer-shorts-as-improvised swimsuit man myself. Indeed, on the afternoon in question, I was wearing an especially fetching white Adidas number with red, white and blue stripes down the side, as worn by my beloved Michel Platini at the European Championships earlier that summer.

But, like everybody else in that Olympic August of 1984, I'd also been enthralled by the wondrous American diver and his ability to somersault so majestically from such great heights.

There was also another crucial difference between us.

In every instance, Louganis was hurtling at great speed and with uncommon grace into beautiful, inviting blue water in warm, sunny Los Angeles, the dramatic contortions of his body always backgrounded by a perfect azure sky. I was standing above a body of black, sinister wet stuff that looked no more welcoming now that the chilly wind was whipping up small waves that crashed with a menacing hiss against the side walls. Not to mention that somewhere high above me lurked the traditional sepia-coloured blanket of clouds that promised and nearly always delivered rain.

I shifted my feet on the concrete platform, searching for better purchase. As if that was going to help. I inhaled deeply again.

From below I could now hear the strains of George Michael belting out 'Careless Whisper' from somebody's boom box. The last thing I needed. The song had only come out a couple of weeks earlier but I was already sick to death of it. It never seemed to be off the radio. Fitting then that it was to be the cringe-worthy soundtrack to my embarrassment as I stood atop the diving platform at the Lee Baths and tried to summon up the courage to dive from the highest point. It wasn't that my guilty feet especially lacked rhythm, it was courage they needed.

I'd rehearsed this moment a thousand times in my head over the previous years. Earlier that morning I lay in bed and decided this would, finally, be the day to dive from the highest perch, and finally fulfil my destiny at the place we referred to almost lovingly as 'The Baths'. I knew exactly how I should look when launching myself into the air too (thank you, Mr Louganis). But, now, now that the moment was at hand, now that I was in the arena, the spotlight on me, I was scared. Make that petrified.

'You better hurry, the lifeguards are coming,' shouted my friend Steve Mehigan from the platform below. He'd given me a leg-up on the last part of the climb because he'd been there before me. He had already made his bones the previous week, something he quite enjoyed reminding me about. All the time. Every day. On the hour. Now I would stop his boasting. Or maybe I wouldn't.

His warning brought renewed urgency to my situation. I glanced over at the lifeguards' house that stood at the top of the deep end of the pool, a place where improbably leather-skinned men and women with pneumatic biceps and mahogany forearms kept watch on our hastily improvised and often barely passable attempts at swimming and diving. There was definitely movement up there all right. Were they really coming for me? Or were they just rearranging the deckchairs because they heard a rumour that the sun might peek out from underneath the clouds and put in its contractually-obliged twice-monthly appearance sometime later that afternoon?

I had no way of knowing. The only thing I knew for certain was that I couldn't climb back down the way I came. That would be a shame too far for any thirteen-year-old boy, especially since I could now hear that a gaggle of giggling girls had joined the audience, hanging around, watching, waiting, anticipating some sort of show. They were also probably wondering, like everybody else, including myself, whether this floppy-haired character really had the guts to fling himself from on high.

I took another deep breath. I think that I secretly hoped each one represented a fresh infusion of bravery or determination. It didn't.

I peeked downward again. The water looked a tad calmer but that didn't help either. It still resembled a sheet of darkness upon which a boy might crack open his skull if the dive went even slightly awry. And that was the other problem here. Just by placing myself in this precarious position, I had contradicted all the warnings given to me by mother since we first were brought to the Lee Baths as toddlers.

Even for a woman with a seemingly endless supply of apocalyptic horror stories designed to dissuade her children from ever taking any risks, her cautionary tale about diving from the top level at 'The Baths' was particularly memorable. It was a graphic account of the day a young boy (his age was never given) plummeted thirty feet and cracked his head open on the side wall of the pool. How did he end up colliding with the concrete? Well, apparently, he dove sideways and a mighty wind blew up at just that precise moment and sent his slight body billowing off course with tragic consequences.

'They had to drain the pool to get the last of his brains out of the water,' she said with the usual flourish she reserved for stories of death, illness and disfigurement.

They had to drain the pool to get the last of his brains out of the water. The kind of line that sticks with you long after you start to figure out the story wasn't actually true. Or at least that no record exists of it happening. And you know this because while researching a school project on Ancient Egypt at the city library one afternoon you had the wit to ask a man behind a desk who looked like he'd know stuff.

'I want to find a story in an old *Evening Echo* about the day a boy smashed his head off the diving board at the Lee Baths and died,' I declared.

'Do you know what year that was?' he asked, deadpan, like this was the sort of inquiry he dealt with all the time.

'No, my mother says it was a while back and they had to drain the pool to get the last of his brains out of the water.'

He took a moment to consider that image. Obviously impressed.

'Listen, boy,' he said, leaning over the desk as if to make sure I heard him, 'there are thousands and thousands of copies of old *Echos* in here and I can tell you now that story isn't in any of them.'

This perplexed me. Surely a 'Boy plunges to bloody, brain-spilling death in public pool' story made the local newspaper.

'Why not?' I asked, seeking more clarification.

'Eh, I think you should ask your mother that,' he replied, easing back into his seat and, for some reason, turning away from me.

At thirteen, I was, thanks to sceptics like the helpful librarian, starting to question the doctrine of maternal infallibility to which I'd subscribed since birth. I still hadn't reached the point where I fully doubted the veracity of my mother's word on everything. Or, at the very least, in certain dangerous situations, I still worried there might, just might, be a kernel of truth to some of her more outlandish tales. That degree of uncertainty was enough to weaken my knees now that I was far above the ground, seeking to follow in the footsteps of the mythical boy who met such a grisly end.

One more breath. Still no intake of courage.

One more glance at the lifeguards. No, they weren't coming to admonish and potentially save me either. Even if a part of me now desperately wished they would arrive in a flurry of authority and order me to abort my plan, allowing me to climb down while blaming those over-officious killjoys for interrupting my daredevil act.

'Are you going or what?'

A voice came from behind and startled me. Another kid had climbed up. A smaller kid. Maybe a foot smaller. A younger kid. Maybe three years younger. Was he ten? No. Could he be nine? Surely not. He was probably just small for his age. I gulped and hoped he didn't see how shocked and impressed I was that somebody so small, so slight, so young had the guts to climb up this high. I hoped he wasn't mature enough to know that his presence had fazed me and, now, unquestionably, without further ado, forced my hand.

'Yeah, yeah, I'm about to go now,' I said, feigning nonchalance, pretending I hadn't been up here for way too long trying to steel myself for the task.

My stomach lurched as I finished the sentence.

'There's no comfort in the truth,' crooned George Michael far below. 'Pain is all you'll find.'

I stepped forward. Rested my feet on the very edge. Half on, half off, just like Louganis. I took another deep breath, filled my chest and…

The Lee Baths was opened by Hugo V. Flinn, TD for Cork Borough and parliamentary secretary to the Minister for Finance, on 20 June 1934. It had cost £23,000 to build, most of which apparently went on wages because, in their wisdom, the city fathers wanted a construction project large enough to provide gainful employment to as many men struggling in the Depression as possible. A facility, then, that was built by the city's poor for the city's poor.

'I hope for many years this pool will be a pool of strength, a pool of healthfulness and open air life for the people of Cork,' said Flinn. 'I have pleasure in congratulating the people of its possession and those who are responsible for it, on the good job they have done; may it remain for a long time one of the proudest possessions of the City of Cork.'

These were optimistic sentiments about a pool without a roof in a city that rarely had a proper summer. Still, for five decades, it appears to have been something of a jewel in the municipal crown, a splendid if rather chilly (nobody had ever talked about heating the water I guess) spot that hosted all manner of swimming galas and diving competitions.

The problem was that by the time I first set foot in the place in the mid-1970s it hadn't been updated from the original design in any significant way. It might have been painted. Occasionally. The diving board may have been replaced a few times. Once a decade? But the place that Flinn opened with such a rhetorical flourish was more or less as he left it when the Hannigans barrelled in through the turnstile gates four decades on.

In photographs of the time, it looks threadbare, paint-peeling, grey (even in the colour shots!) and impressively dreary. Of course, that's what I think now. Back then, between the ages of five and fifteen, it was the epicentre of my summer universe, the most wonderful place in our (admittedly) small world.

On television shows like *Hart to Hart* and *Magnum, P.I.*, swimming pools always looked aqua blue, the water inevitably glistening in the sunshine. Even on the sunniest of days – and those were few and far between – the water at the Lee Baths was the black side of grey. It had the murky darkness you encounter near the ocean floor by the Mariana Trench except this was in four feet of water and the floor beneath our bare feet was made of concrete. And of course we were in love with it. We hurtled into its Stygian depths like it was an infinity pool stretching off a cliff beside a scorching Malibu mansion.

No matter that the moment we plunged in, the bitter cold of the water zipped through us, shocking every nerve ending for a few seconds. On a really bad day (which was most of them), you quickly felt a sharp pain in both knees. But, then, somehow, after we stopped pretending we couldn't breathe, our bodies acclimatised to the Arctic conditions. There must be a curious sort of mechanism in a child's body that causes excitement to obviate physical discomfort. Within a minute we splashed about delightedly, suddenly oblivious to the fact this was as cold as the cold tap in a house without central heating on a frosty January morning.

Except it was mid-July and outside.

We loved it because we knew no better. It was only later we discovered indoor pools where the water was, gasp, heated. Such an exotic place existed out in Douglas, the other side of town, the other side of our planet. That was a strange, unfriendly facility where they charged too much and allowed you swim too little. They frowned upon you doing cannonballs, berated you for what martinet lifeguards called 'horseplay'. But worst of all, they emptied the pool every 55 minutes and made you leave so a fresh batch of suckers could come in.

Swimming in the Gus Healy Pool in Douglas also involved strange, discomfiting rituals. These entailed washing your feet on the way into the water (who had ever heard of such a thing?) and rubbing the chlorine out of your eyes the whole way home.

These modern affectations and sops to basic hygiene we might have tolerated except on most days getting in there usually involved queuing up for an hour to swim less than an hour. A ridiculous arrangement when compared to the bounty of the Lee Baths.

In our al fresco slice of heaven, you could hang around all day and if you did, your persistence was rewarded. You got to witness the lifeguards dragging out goalposts so men with v-shaped torsos and skull caps could play an especially violent brand of water polo, some strange amalgam of fisticuffs and exaggerated splashing. We sat poolside, mesmerised by the spectacle, Corkonian plebeians baying for the gladiators to spill blood.

A trail of crimson in the water was not an unusual sight in the Lee Baths at any time of day. Walking into the shallow end your toe might snag on a jagged edge of the stone that lay beneath your feet. An uneven patch of ground could open your sole and produce blood. Over time, like tribes that run barefoot on all terrain, the regulars got used to it, our skin toughened like leather and we became inured to these inconsistencies.

Picking microscopic pebbles from your feet after you left the water was just part of the experience. All good, not so clean fun. We didn't know that the bottom surface of a pool was usually smooth and lined. How could we when this was the first pool we ever entered?

This peculiar feature was not to everybody's liking. Arrivistes often resorted to swimming with their shoes on to stave off the inevitable pain of these injuries. Not swimming shoes. Not plastic sandals or flip flops. Actual runners, sometimes even with their socks still on. This was a fool's errand though. Later, we'd spot these bluffers regretting their decision as they squelched and sloshed their way along Victoria Cross, water spraying out the sides of their shoes with every sad footfall. Their faces also betrayed their growing dread of what their mothers might do to them when they got home.

There were other distinctive touches to the place too. The doors on the changing cubicles didn't lock. I'm not sure who decided this. I never figured out whether it was by accident or by dint of some bizarre engineering design. They were like one half of those saloon doors you see in westerns, forever swinging in the ubiquitous breeze. The absence of any way of keeping the door properly closed created unique challenges and certain playful opportunities.

For instance, some kids liked to amuse themselves by running the length of the walkways pushing every single door in for a lark. This was hilarious to watch unless you were inside one of those cubicles at the time, trying to put your Y-front underpants back on. Nothing is less funny than being knocked off balance by a hefty wooden door smacking you in the head when you have only one leg in your undies. Especially if you shriek rather than bellow and fall to the ground in a crumpled heap so people outside get a full glimpse of your mostly nude pre-pubescent body while simultaneously hearing the high-pitched wails of your discomfort. It's difficult to come back from that.

Again, this was where regulars had an advantage over the day-trippers. From a young age, you knew to be lightning quick in the dressing-room. Or to risk being mortified. If getting into your togs in a confined space while under fear of imminent attack by a pack of feral boys had been an Olympic sport, several of us were surely gold medal contenders.

You also knew that each of your travelling party stashed your clothes together in the same dressing-room, a dressing-room that one of you could see at all times, because the Lee

Baths was notorious for thievery. It was not unknown to see a boy walk in with new runners and leave two hours later in his bare feet, skipping gingerly along the footpath as his friends simultaneously sympathised and mocked his plight.

'Watch out for bowsies!' cautioned my mother every time she waved us on our way.

That she was sending a little boy of five or six off into the wild with his older siblings, to trek two miles along some of Cork's busiest roads, wasn't even a consideration for her or any other parent. After all, when they looked out their windows on any half-decent summer day they saw legions of kids of all ages, strolling purposefully along, rolled-up towels beneath their arms. Occasionally, there'd be a multi-tasking mother from Togher Road pushing a pram, a she-wolf herding her playful cubs along at fierce pace, all part of the great urban migration towards water.

The journey itself was a minor epic. If we were feeling brave we'd cut through Schoolboy's Lane, a secluded dirt path between fields and trees that abutted the Presentation Brothers' School's impeccably laid-out rugby fields. A secluded dirt path that we later discovered was perfectly appointed for illicit teenage drinking sessions. A secluded dirt path where a rival group of kids could take umbrage at your presence and attack.

Aside from the off-chance of violent reprisals by other boys menacingly wielding towels, there was also the risk of running into a new urban species, the glue-sniffers. For a time in the 1980s, Ireland suffered this very peculiar epidemic when gaggles of teens hung around the streets like zombies, holding plastic bags full of solvents up to their pimpled faces; too out of it to threaten anybody, doing irreparable damage to their own brains.

The other problem with opting for that particular route was it required an almost mandatory stop to visit the ruins of the old Glasheen Boys' National School. Half an hour of valuable swimming time could be wasted just exploring the dilapidated shells of former classrooms, eyes on the floor, hoping to stumble across some sort of treasure. We never found anything except empty beer bottles and discarded flagons, but that never seemed to discourage us from trying anew.

That particular way shaved about a mile off the walk though and, once we hit Dennehy's pub it was, literally, all downhill from there until we reached Victoria Cross. By that point anticipation was building. Upon taking the final left turn into the Carrigrohane Straight, we discovered just how chilly the breeze was going to be. And there was always a breeze. Even on the stillest of days, a wind whipped up that road like it had been mustering strength since it set off from the Angler's Rest three miles earlier.

Just before reaching the gates, the bigger kids handed us their towels and togs and set off on reconnaissance missions to find ways to climb over the wall without being detected. In my earliest memory of this practice, the admission fee was two pence, but getting in free was a challenge to their ingenuity and courage, not to mention good for all our pockets. As a young child, it was a great (and perhaps slightly unfair) responsibility to be carrying four older boys' towels and four pairs of togs about your person as you stumbled along, hoping the lifeguard manning the entrance didn't ask why you were laden down like a Sherpa leaving base camp.

Once inside, the rendezvous point was behind the toilets. A discreet location, so discreet in fact that it was also where, when fights inevitably broke out, most of the hand-to-hand combat between boys (and on a few occasions girls too) took place.

It was there, out of sight of the authorities, that those who had vaulted over the walls for free had to share the money they saved with their junior accomplices. Then we all made a quick stop at the Lee Baths' concession stand. Well, it was more of a table really, manned by a formidable mother and daughter team who brooked no messing as we pored over the cornucopia of chocolate and drinks on offer. Any brave fool who dared to ask 'How much are the penny bars?' received a withering stare and, depending on their mood, might even be refused service altogether.

At one point, the selection of beverages on offer included 'Super' cans of Coca-Cola, one and a half times the regular size. A tremendous idea; the one thing the working class kids of Cork needed was to imbibe a potent mix of caffeine and sugar to absolute excess. No wonder there were so many fights.

When (definitely not if) we ran out of money, everybody kept their eyes peeled for a relation. To meet an aunt or an uncle in 'The Baths' was always a boon. They foisted all manner of goodies upon us, for no other reason than that they were related to us. If they were feeling especially generous, they might even press a few coins into our hands and we'd sprint straight back to the 'shop' for the Macaroon bar or the can of Tanora (a tangerine-flavoured drink only sold in Cork) that we so desperately craved.

It's not that our mother didn't send us off suitably equipped with food. We never left home without jam sandwiches packed in tin-foil, with the crusts carefully clipped off. As requested.

The diet may explain why we spent so many hours having

inane conversations and arguments about bizarre topics that nobody could really win. The Baths sat right next to the County Hall, the unimaginatively named, spectacularly ugly 17-storey office block that was the closest thing we had to a skyscraper. We laid our towels down to lie on (an act known as 'balming out'), and stared up at this building's great height and then the discussion inevitably started.

'Could someone dive off the roof of the County Hall and land in the deep end and survive?'

Rare is the national parliament that had debates as robust or elongated as ours as we tried to figure out whether some daredevil might or might not splatter upon entry. It says much about our extensive knowledge of basic physics that some of us (myself included) were, for the longest time, convinced that any diver entering the water hands first in the perfect Louganis posture could survive the initial impact.

'His fingers would break his fall!' I argued, regularly, vehemently, confident in my ignorance.

In our minds, at least some of the magic surrounding 'The Baths' was the location, sandwiched between so many local landmarks. The County Hall, the tallest building in Cork, the second tallest building in Ireland, on one side of it. On the other, just across the River Lee, Our Lady's Hospital insane asylum stretched along the green hills; dark, gothic and menacing. People who went in there didn't come out, we were told. But never mind that, of much more import to us was the place's unique claim to fame. According to my father and my uncles and my grandfather and just about every adult male in Cork that I knew, Our Lady's boasted the longest corridor in Europe.

I'm not sure how this was ascertained. Was there a corridor commission that evaluated such things? Had a deputation from Brussels visited Cork and officially signed off on this outrageous assertion? Or, was it, as I suspect now with the passing of time, a local legend? In any case, it was all grist to the mill of our sense of Corkonian superiority. The longest corridor in all of Europe!

Gleefully, we dined out on such local legends and gorged on urban myths for dessert. Boys at school were adamant that the Lee Baths was a no-go area because they'd heard from a friend of a friend of a cousin's brother that conger eels lived in the deep end. Conger eels. Not trout. Not salmon. Conger eels. One of the more vicious-looking sea creatures to inhabit Irish waters. We'd never actually seen one in person, but I had found a single disturbing photograph of one when I went sifting through a fishing book in Ballyphehane library.

So the story went, the conger eels swum into the baths through the piping that connected it to the river next door. That sounded plausible enough except we never saw any critter no matter how deep we dived, no matter the quality of the goggles we wore. The water was surely too filthy for any beast to survive and if there were fish in there we never saw them. And we looked. And looked. And looked. We whiled away hours throwing bottle tops into the six feet section and diving to retrieve them from the bottom like the Corkonian Jacques Cousteaus we fancied ourselves to be.

Still, I was perturbed enough about the possibility of a conger eel biting my face to raise the issue with my father.

'Do you think there are conger eels in the deep end?' I asked.

'No, boy,' he replied.

'But how can you be sure?'

He paused and with a perfectly straight face, answered, 'Because they'd be afraid some of the swimmers might bite them back.'

I groped for the heavy metal ladder and then hoisted myself onto the bottom rung. Once my head emerged from the water, I did the exaggerated headshake I'd noticed all the Olympic divers were fond of doing upon leaving the pool. The mannerism of a showboater. A showboater who'd failed to deliver a show.

'You funked it, boy!' I didn't know the voice. I didn't look up to see the face. The person putting me in my place was right on the money.

I funked it. I completely and utterly funked it. At the last moment, I panicked, straightened my body up and jumped off feet first.

I had, indeed, funked it.

I climbed the ladder and started to rush away from the scene of the crime. But I couldn't. A huge crowd had gathered and my path was blocked. I turned to see what they were looking at. I saw the little boy who had queued up behind me. He was flying through the air, holding perfect Louganis form, and all around the diving pool there was the sound of impressed gasping followed by an outbreak of appreciative clapping.

TWO

Ball Games

My Auntie Kathleen lived around the corner from us in Maple Place. She had just had her second baby, a boy named Robert. In lieu of frankincense or myrrh, some less than wise man had gifted the new child a soccer ball. Not a soft-toy-type thing that could be put in his crib. An actual soccer ball. I'd seen it up there in his room, on the floor between the rocking chair and the crib. I'd noticed how pristine and perfect it looked and I was envious from the moment I set eyes upon it.

How could it be anything less than spotless though? Small Rob, as he'd be known even after he grew to over six feet, was only a few months old. Yet one of his uncles had given him a white ball with the word 'United' printed on one of its rectangular panels. A cute acknowledgement of the fact his Liverpool-supporting father was sports-mad and, by his own hilariously exaggerated, impossible to believe but hugely entertaining account, a wonderful Gaelic footballer too.

I was insanely jealous, both of the new baby getting so much attention and him being the proud owner of a ball without a single blemish on it. Especially so because this coincided with a downturn in the fortunes of our street.

For a period of what must have been days, but felt like weeks, during the sweltering summer of 1977, nobody living in or near our square owned a functioning ball. We had lost or destroyed every single one we owned, a couple falling victim to merciless cars and trucks trundling too fast along Clashduv Road. In a time when parents didn't and couldn't shop on demand for sporting goods, this put a temporary stop to our soccer-playing. And left a gaping hole in our young lives.

Sure, we improvised a bit. Somebody found a tennis ball out in their shed and we tried that for a time one day but the problem with a ball that small is your touch has to be really, really good to make it fun. We were not at that level. Soccer tennis of that particular kind got old quick when basic control was beyond our ken.

On one particular afternoon, a gang of us were sitting on the curb lamenting our terrible misfortune, trying to dream up scenarios through which we might source even a deflated ball that we could knock around. That's when I mentioned my baby cousin Robert's beautiful white ball for which he had no actual use.

Immediately, I came under pressure. We were related. They were bound to give it to me.

'What about you, Tom?' I asked my brother, older by three years and also part of the group. 'Why don't you go ask?'

'No, it's better if you do it.'

'Why?'

''Cause you're six is why!'

I resisted at first but quickly gave in. Another long, hot afternoon stretching before us without a ball was much less appetising than an afternoon with one. Accompanied by everybody else, and feeling just a little bit more significant than usual, I trudged along Clashduv Road, and up the small hill of

Whitebeam Road until we reached the entrance to Maple Place. There, the rest of them suddenly stopped.

One of the older boys gave me a quick tutorial on how to do proper puppy-dog eyes (the only part I remembered was bowing my head) and then they sent me on my way. I had to conduct the final leg of my mission alone.

With sweaty palms, I knocked on the door of the downstairs flat my relatives called home. Doorbells were a gentrification that had yet to make their way into our neighbourhood. My Auntie Kathleen answered. She wore the frazzled look of a young mother juggling children and too much to do.

'Can I have a lend of baby Robert's soccer ball?' I blurted, giving it my best puppy-dog eyes though she scarcely seemed to notice the affectation.

'What?' she asked.

'The baby's ball. Can I borrow it?'

'What ball?'

'You know the one in his bedroom. By the wall.'

She had no idea what I was even talking about. What type of person doesn't even notice a perfectly good, beautiful new ball?

Suddenly her daughter appeared from the hallway. Rachel. Also six. My cousin. My sometime friend. My often nemesis. With the very ball in her hands.

'Is this what you want?' she asked in a slightly peevish tone that made me think she was going to use it to tease me.

'Yes, yes it is.'

Kathleen turned, took it from her and handed it over. 'Mind it now and bring it back when you're finished.'

'Thanks. Thanks. Thanks. I will.'

I held it under my right oxter until I reached the corner where my friends and older brother were still standing sentry. Then, I lifted it above my head. In triumph. I had delivered the boys of

Clashduv Road from the prison of boredom. I had ended our soccer-ball-less hell. I had procured a perfect, white ball for our entertainment. We tumbled down the hill for home, shrieking and hollering with unbridled joy, desperate to start a game.

Just minutes later, I realised that my main contribution to the festivities was already over. When the teams were picked, I was last to be chosen. The curse of the youngest kid on the block. As a six-year-old, I was afforded no special privileges in any street match. Ever. Even if my ingenuity and familial connections had just made the whole thing possible with my stealthy mission up to Auntie Kathleen's. You got what you deserved in our games.

If you won the ball, well and good; if you didn't, you stood around a lot and watched others do wondrous stuff with it. When you were giving away years to many of your opponents, as I was that day, you took the only wise option available. You became a sneaky-liner. A bottom feeder. You hung around the goal your team was attacking, waiting to feed on scraps from bigger players, lucky rebounds or mistakes by the keeper.

When my brother Tom happened to be on my team and was in one of his more charitable moods, he might set me up with a gilt-edged opportunity in front of goal. If I failed to convert the chance he'd bollock me and swear never to assist me again. This was a tough, uncompromising environment where you learned to scrap for the ball or you soon decided playing wasn't worth the effort. Years before we learned about Charles Darwin, we lived his credo.

Our square was an arena without referees and with few rules. That you might end up being unfairly dumped on the gravel after attempting and failing to dispossess boys nearly twice your age was merely part of the culture. Picking tiny stones out of a cut in your knee was just an especially painful and painstaking facet of this sporting education and maturation. The kind of unfortunate side effect that the English public schools system might have filed under 'character-forming experience'.

When our game ended that particular day, I brought the ball inside to the kitchen. I found a tea towel that I wet under the tap and then I assiduously wiped the surface back towards something approaching its original whiteness. I saw the U on United was already starting to peel and hoped my aunt wouldn't notice. Not realising, of course, that she wouldn't see it or care. Before I set off on the return leg of the journey to her house, I went looking for others to accompany me but the street was empty.

'Where is everybody gone?' I asked Tom.

'They've all gone home.'

'Will you walk up to Kathleen's with me to bring back the ball?'

'No,' he said, grinning. 'You got it, you have to bring it back.'

Another lesson learned about my place in the food chain of the street.

I can't pinpoint the exact moment I started to question the existence of Santa Claus, but I know exactly the year I began to have doubts. On Christmas morning 1978, Tom, my sisters Anne and Denise, and I crept downstairs long before dawn. As was the annual routine. Being the eldest, Denise prised open the living room door, and flicked on the light switch. Then we poured in behind her to marvel at the largesse of the fat man in the red coat and white beard.

There, underneath the tree, resplendent in all its glory, was a wonderful orange soccer ball. When we liberated it from the box, we discovered there was a Johan Cruyff autograph etched in black across one of the panels. It hadn't been on my list. It hadn't been on Tommy's either. But we both knew that there was somebody in our lives with a deep, abiding appreciation for Dutch football and a serious obsession with its finest exponent. And it wasn't Santa.

It was the man who came downstairs moments later, bleary-eyed, and pretended to be shocked when he saw us cradling this ball. A ball that just happened to be emblazoned with the name of his favourite footballer ever.

Earlier that year, my father had broken his ankle, following an abortive attempt to show his kids how to perform the Cruyff drag-back in a caravan park in Owenahincha. He had almost pulled it off when his left foot stuck in the ground at just the wrong moment. He hobbled to a neighbour's car, wounded but unbowed, and was driven away to the city as darkness fell over the nearby Atlantic Ocean. I was never prouder of him. When it came to preaching the gospel of Cruyff, he never missed a chance to take to the pulpit.

The 1978 World Cup in Argentina was the first tournament I was old enough to enjoy. It was a landmark event in the history of our house – our first colour television arrived a week before it began. As thick as it was tall, the Nordmende with the 26-inch screen was meant to accentuate our enjoyment of the games and to make up for the absence of Cruyff from the Dutch squad. He may have refused to travel to South America but his ghost loomed large in our lives for those weeks.

Every time we sat down to watch the Netherlands my father reiterated the reason Cruyff had stayed at home. And so it was at the tender age of seven I learned the meaning of the crucial phrase 'military junta'. That it later emerged the Dutchman's reasons for not travelling weren't solely based on conscientious objection is neither here nor there. I grew up believing Cruyff was different in so many ways than every other player. My father had many, many ways of proving this.

Once I remember him showing us a photograph of Cruyff playing goalkeeper in training, diving full length to clutch a ball with both hands. 'See that, he can play anywhere!'

It was another blow to the family that summer when Wim Van Hanegem opted out of the Dutch squad before they flew to Argentina because, at thirty-four, he was no longer guaranteed a starting spot. My father used to love to claim that the bandy-legged midfielder was one of our cousins from the Netherlands.

'Don't be telling anybody that but it's true,' he whispered.

His secret was safe with me. I told everybody I met that summer!

It was a tournament where my sporting and geographical education intensified. I learned new countries, Iran and Tunisia, and the names of so many wonderful players: Peru's Teófilo Cubillas, Brazil's Zico and Austria's Hans Krankl. Of course, that June these giants of the sport were all only considered warm-up acts at 66 Clashduv Road, where the lack of Cruyff hadn't diminished my father's love for the Dutch. And so I too became besotted by Messrs Neeskens, Rep, Haan, Rensenbrink and the Van der Kerkhof twins.

For my father it wasn't just about enjoying the quality of their play either. He was also on a quest to make me understand the larger significance of sport and how it intersects with all aspects of society and life. Or, as he put it in language I could understand:

'Never trust the Germans, boy!'

'Why?'

'They robbed the Dutch four years ago.'

'Oh.'

'And, you know the Kaiser gassed my father!'

'The Kaiser?'

'He was, like, the Emperor of Germany in World War I.'

I nodded because this sounded a little too much like school and I wanted him to stop. I later discovered Kaiser Wilhelm II hadn't personally sprayed my grandfather with chemical weapons at the Somme. But some of the soldiers fighting in his name definitely did. And that was enough for my dad to nurse a healthy suspicion of all Germans for all of his life, a distrust amplified by West Germany's triumph over the Netherlands in the 1974 World Cup final. Even after the Berlin Wall came down, every German team was subject to being denounced and wished ill-fortune.

When Argentina finally edged ahead of the Dutch in the 1978 final, my father was distraught (this, I later discovered, may also have had something to do with him having bet money on the Netherlands). He was certain that Cruyff's presence would have made all the difference and that the home team had benefited from some dodgy refereeing. That night, I added words like 'fix' and 'corruption' to my burgeoning vocabulary.

That a Cruyff football managed to find its way from the North Pole to the southside of Cork just six months later was no coincidence. Santa obviously wanted to offer a consolation prize to make sure our devotion to the Oranje didn't wane. Later, brilliant orange Adidas t-shirts with three black stripes on each arm and a suede version of the lion of the Dutch Republic on the left breast were added to our wardrobes, ensuring we kept the faith.

The problem with the ball we received that Christmas is that the autograph, however it was machine printed, started to fade once we began to use it. Quickly. Especially when the ball was being bounced around on a concrete surface. By the time we went back to school in early January, the Johan Cruyff football looked just like any other beaten-up orange football. All signs that it had once received the imprimatur of the apostle of total football had long since been consigned to history. Like my belief in Santa.

Mr Healy stood up from his desk with a folder in his hand, calling fifth class to order. Then he started to talk rather strangely about milk and cows and all matters dairy. We were bemused until he announced that there was to be an essay-writing competition sponsored by An Bord Bainne: The Milk Board. My ears pricked up. I could write. At least I thought I could. I was ten, too young to spell hubris, old enough to feel it.

And I'd heard of this competition before. I'd been waiting for this day since my older brother had come home three years earlier with the eyes-widening story of the boy in his class who won first prize – an actual, real, authentic leather soccer ball. Or, as we called it, a leathera.

I sat up straighter in my chair as the teacher continued his lecture. Slides of cows and farms and milk floats flashed up on the screen from the overhead projector. The way that I remember that phase of my education is that there were always slides about something. On this day, it just happened to be milk and cows. Cows and milk. To suburban kids who'd only ever seen farms blurring past our car windows on the way to the seaside in summer, this was dull and boring and badly in need of somebody livening it up. I was going to be that somebody.

At some point, Mr Healy started to explain the milking process and, over a visual of an old woman coaxing milk from a cow's udders into a bucket, he uttered the word 'teat'. He moved on swiftly but I couldn't. That four-letter word was all it took. I dissolved into a laughter so organic I didn't even bother to try to stifle it. Teat. It sounded almost like, well, you know…

It was as if somebody had tickled my funny bone. The giggling was uncontrollable and contagious enough that it soon spread, rippling its way around the room. Had the others found it funny too? Or were they laughing at me laughing? Or were they guffawing at how angry Mr Healy now looked? Possibly all of the above.

He stopped speaking, put away his script, and bore down on my desk. Plenty of others had joined in the merry chorus as it grew, but he knew I was the instigator of the whole kerfuffle. I was the boy in the sights of one very angry teacher.

Funny thing is, I wasn't the class clown. I hadn't the courage or the wit to fulfill that role. I left the jokes that cracked up the room and tormented Mr Healy to braver and sharper kids. Well, until this day.

There were no violent reprisals. Mr Healy wasn't like that. He was a wonderful teacher, if not, on this particular day, one inclined to tolerate any juvenile carry-on from me. As was his wont with miscreants, he simply sent me from the room. A cursory wave of his right hand towards the door. His version of the red card. I slinked off the field, my head now slumped into my shoulders, my cheeks reddening at the embarrassing nature of my dismissal. I was bang to rights. It didn't enter my head to protest the decision. I knew the rules. I broke them. I had to pay the price.

While my classmates spent the next hour learning more and more and more about milk and the dairy industry, I stewed outside in the corridor. My own private prison. I leaned against the wall like a weary lag wishing the end of his sentence would come quicker. I distracted myself by goofing around, swinging out of the nearby coat racks, every Lord Anthony jacket inevitably damp and smelling of rain. At the sound of footsteps, I drew one of them around me and hid lest I be discovered by the principal, Mr Lynch. I did not want to explain the nature of my offence to a higher power.

Mostly, though, I just seethed out there because I wanted to win that competition. Badly. Sure, milk was about as dull a subject as I could imagine but here was a chance to take home a new soccer ball. A leathera. That opportunity trumped everything. On Clashduv Road we had kicked every type of sphere around in our street games, but never, ever, a proper leather football.

How badly did I covet one? Sometimes, when my mother would get groceries at Roches Stores in the Wilton Shopping Centre, she'd deposit me at the door of Lifestyle Sports. There, I'd often stand in front of the leather balls, for both soccer and Gaelic football, that they had perched on holders attached to the wall. They were up there almost like trophies.

If no one was looking I might take one down, bounce it on the floor, and squeeze it between my hands the way goalies did before launching it down the field. Very occasionally, I'd even hold it up to my face and smell it. Only occasionally. I didn't want anybody working there to think I was weird or anything. I was just a kid who dreamed of one day owning a leathera of his own.

Now, it looked like I'd blown my chance to do just that. As the duration of my exile lengthened, I began to seriously worry that I might be prohibited from even entering the competition. It was not a thought I wanted to entertain yet the more I ruminated about it the more I realised Mr Healy would be entitled to do just that. After all, I knew soccer players in

England got banned from subsequent matches after every red card. Would the same justice system apply here?

I worried unduly. Mr Healy was a fair man. Once I was reintegrated back into the general population that day, he handed me the same hefty booklet of government-sponsored dairy propaganda that he'd given to everybody else. I was back in the game. Indeed, I was back in the game with a heightened sense of purpose, like an embittered sub who'd missed out on the opportunity to start. Now, I was a frustrated player determined to prove the manager wrong, more up than ever to pen something about milk.

It mattered little that the sum of my knowledge of the liquid was this – I hated the sight, smell and chalky taste of the stuff, especially when it came in the subsidized cartons given to us by the school. I hated that cow juice almost as much as I loved the thought of one day owning my own leathera. I wrote and wrote and wrote.

Weeks passed. Maybe months. Enough time anyway that I'd completely forgotten about milk and essays about it. Then one damp morning (in my memory they were all damp and overcast), Mr Healy beckoned me out of the classroom to the corridor. The same place I'd spent my quarantine during his bovine lecture. This time though, the mood was different. He was smiling before he even started speaking. I could see in his hands a slim, glossy brochure of some kind. He held it up as if in affirmation and he said, 'You won.'

I have no memory of what I even wrote in that essay. I just know I wrote enough to convince some judge somewhere that mine was better than everybody else's in the class.

'Have a look through that,' he said, beaming as he handed over a catalogue showing a host of prizes selected by An Bord Bainne.

I only recall two of the items on offer. At least I only had eyes for two that day: a soccer ball and a camera. In my house in 1981 we didn't have a working camera. There was a damaged Polaroid Instamatic that had been put on a bookshelf in the living room a couple of Christmases earlier after causing too much frustration when it kept malfunctioning. But that was more or less it when it came to photographic equipment and the Hannigans.

Briefly, I considered opting for the camera. Very briefly. We were not the kind of family that captured every significant moment on film. We were the kind who stood reluctantly and stiffly for portrait photographers in breezy church yards before First Holy Communion and Confirmation ceremonies. My father had watched too many Westerns and read enough Zane Grey novels to regularly trot out the old line about Native Americans believing every photograph stole a little from your soul. He seemed to take his lead from that. He was obviously part-Cherokee from way back.

'I want the ball, please,' I said, after taking all of maybe 45 seconds to think it over.

'Wise decision,' replied Mr Healy. He wasn't surprised. He coached us in Gaelic football in his spare time and the very first week I sat in his class I impressed him by naming the Celtic goalscorers (Tommy Gemmell and Stevie Chalmers) in the 1967 European Cup final. He knew my inclinations.

The ball arrived two weeks later. It had black and white octagonal patches, and it was as beautiful as I'd imagined it when going to sleep each night dreaming of its arrival. There was no brand name on it. Never mind. I was too young to care about that or to know what it signified regarding quality and the price. It mattered only that it was black and white and greatly resembled the ball caressed and pinged about by Pelé and his pals in the *Giants of Brazil* video that I'd recently seen at my Uncle Eddie's house over in Ballyphehane. And it mattered that it was leather. A leathera.

Well, what I thought was leather at the time. It was actually some sort of synthetic fibre, a kind of ersatz leather, but, hey, when you're ten the style is much more important than the substance. And, unlike every other ball we used to hone our talents, it wasn't made of an especially unforgiving version of hard industrial plastic. This was almost like a real ball.

'We can only use this on grass,' I declared to my friends that day. 'Otherwise, we'll ruin it.'

It is a measure of how much we prized new things that everybody agreed with this stipulation. A boon like this was indeed to be treasured. Knocking it about on the harsh, stony surface of the concrete square that abutted our houses and hadn't yet been colonised for car parking would shred the ball in weeks. Using it on grass would prolong its life for who knows how long. Maybe until one of the younger kids on the road could win a future edition of the essay contest.

And the ball did last. We had it through the 1982 World Cup and, it remained stubbornly inflated and usable even when the 1984 European Championships came around. At various points in its life span, when the black and white patches began to peel and fade, I tried to stave off the tell-tale signs of ageing and overuse.

I sat at the kitchen table one night with a heavy black marker that I'd found in my sisters' room and a bottle of Tipp-Ex correctional fluid. With the determination of somebody attempting to restore a great work of art, I tried to colour the ball back into something resembling its original beauty and almost got high from inhaling the fumes.

My restoration job succeeded too – at least until the first time we kicked it around again and the 'new' coat came off on our shoes. After that, I never tried to clean it up again, accepting that it was to see out its days with every patch turned eventually to darkest grey, the colour transformation a fitting monument to how many hours it had served us.

And it served us, oh, so well. It felt different from the notoriously hard plastic balls we lashed around the square. It stayed inflated longer and it didn't have difficult ridges on it like the David O'Leary ball that Texaco offered to get our fathers to buy their petrol by collecting stamps in a book. The leathera seemed easier to juggle and felt gentler on the head. It was, as we kept reminding ourselves every time we contemplated its magnificence, almost like a real ball. Like they'd use in a real game. Maybe that's why we persuaded ourselves it made us play better.

We ran into difficulties that the professionals we worshipped never encountered. One of our favourite venues for the leathera was a swatch of green that stretched the length of Riverview Estate. It was perfect for soccer because some of the trees that grew there had thick trunks that made for ideal goalposts. Even better, there was a six-foot metal fence behind the trees. If you scored, the ball rebounded directly off it and right into your path. No running miles to fetch it. Of course, that was if you scored…

If you didn't score and the goalie didn't save it, there was a chance the ball would fly over the fence and right into the Glasheen Stream that meandered by on the other side of the barrier. That's where the trouble started. That's where we turned into intrepid bounty hunters, running along the riverbank, hurdling fallen branches like tribesmen in this urban jungle, trying to find a dry spot from which the escaping ball might be corralled and returned to safety.

Sometimes, the ball got stuck in the weeds or the debris that made this one of those down-at-heel suburban Irish waterways never destined to attract tourists or feature in the pages of glossy magazines. An upturned shopping cart here. The front seat of a Ford Capri there. The detritus was varied and colourful and bloody annoying for aspiring soccer players needing to rescue a ball fast drifting away to obscurity. Or wherever the stream went after it passed under the small bridge that led to St Finbarr's hurling and football club.

These sorts of obstacles ensured that there were days we spent more time hunting in the river than we did kicking the ball. Which may also explain why none of us ever made it to the top. Either that or we just didn't have any talent.

In any case, there was one particular evening when the stream wouldn't give up the ball. We spent an hour trying and failing to reach it. But it was too far from the bank, strangled in a fresh crop of weeds. Reluctantly, we headed home, deflated, defeated, deprived of our beloved leathera, still assuring each other that we'd return the next morning to restart the rescue effort.

Morning broke wet and windy. Nobody was going anywhere to search for a ball. The rain continued. The wait went on. At one point, I was standing in the living room, staring out the window at the relentless showers, wondering, as usual, whether the dark clouds on the hill up towards the airport were on their way in or out. That's when I thought I saw it. A leathera that looked suspiciously like my leathera – I'd know the missing patches of white and black anywhere – in the possession of a kid from the flats next door as he sheltered from the rain in the stairwell of that complex.

I wiped the condensation from the glass and pressed my nose closer for a better look. No doubt about it. That wasn't any ball. It was my ball. My leathera. This boy was a year younger than me. I'd never had any run-ins with him. But, at that moment, it wouldn't have mattered if he'd have been ten feet tall and the toughest kid in Togher (a title for which there was some serious competition). I ran out of the house. No coat. Nothing. Angry enough to be oblivious to the driving rain. There was no great confrontation. I just blurted out words and grabbed my ball. He offered no protest. He knew it was mine.

I stormed back into the house, placed the ball safely by the back door in the kitchen. My mother shouted at me for making the floor wet and dirty, but I scarcely heard anything because my heart was thumping with excitement. The ball was back in its proper place. All was right with the world. Soon after that, the kid, like many of our neighbours, moved from the flats to a freshly-built Cork Corporation house out in Bishopstown. I never did get to ask him how he had got the ball. Had he stomped the riverbank in the rain? Had he seen me and my friends give up the ghost the previous night and nipped in as soon as we left? Had he walked into the water just to grab it?

However he did it, he'd shown the kind of enterprise in tough circumstances that demonstrated just what a truly great prize a leathera was.

THREE

Read All About It

Every car journey to my father's family home in Blarney Street took us across the city and always had the potential to turn into a trip through myth and legend. We drove up Togher Road and past The Lough, where we heard once more the tale of the princess who left the spring of life unlocked until her father's kingdom was suddenly underwater.

'It's there even now, beneath The Lough,' he assured us – on cue – every time!

Nearer town, a stop at the traffic lights by St Fin Barre's Cathedral inevitably prompted him to point out 'The Goldy Angel', a six-foot statue perched just below the daunting Gothic spires. My siblings and I gazed up at its shimmering beauty as if God himself had reached down and placed it there. Perhaps encouraged by us being awestruck, my father unfurled the sort of apocalyptic story guaranteed to get our attention.

'When that Angel blows those two horns in her hands, that's it, curtains, the signal the world is about to end!'

All questions about how an inanimate object was going to come to life in order to play that Doomsday tune were dismissed with a gloomy riposte.

'You'll know exactly how when you hear the first notes!'

While studying for my confirmation and boning up on all matters ecclesiastical, I asked him why a Protestant church had been chosen as the place to announce the end of the world. The question stumped him. He fobbed me off. I never asked it again.

On Wandesford Quay, traffic always backed up along the humped back of Clarke's Bridge. There, we were ordered to strain our necks out the window to take in the marvellous, stately sight of George the Lion. Another statue, this time of the king of the jungle, that, for some unknown reason, stood atop the old Millwright House on the corner.

'Why is he called George?' we'd ask.

'Never mind that,' said my father, refusing to admit he didn't know. 'I hear he growls when nobody is looking or listening.'

When we reached The Marsh, the warren of inner city laneways where my mother grew up, we'd drop her off so she could shop on North Main Street while our journey continued northward to his homeland overlooking the town. Upon crossing the River Lee's north channel, the border, my father always perked up. A native returning to his own place, he'd usually mutter something about the clock on top of Shandon, his beloved four-faced liar. The prodigal, or at the very least, the northsider long since exiled to the southside by marriage, coming back.

Every landmark in and around Blarney Street held a story. The orchard on Strawberry Hill where he went slogging apples and lost a new jumper when it snagged on a branch as he made his escape from the irate house owner. The bullet marks on the wall up by Banjo's pub where the unarmed IRA man Denis

Spriggs was executed without trial by British soldiers during the War of Independence, a neighbour ('a black-hearted bastard!') informing them of his whereabouts.

The Hannigan home at number 138 was built into the side of the hill, which made it look like it was crouching low onto the street. There was no doorbell or knocker. If we were calling early on in the morning, my father simply took off his shoe, stepped on the lower window sill and rapped on one of the top panes. My maiden aunts Charlotte and Mary shared one bedroom; my bachelor uncles Bobby and Mick another. They all lived in the house where they grew up, and they all showered us with kindness and largesse during our visits. We never once left their company without a stack of coins and sometimes even notes being pressed into our hands.

It was an old house. Up until the mid-1980s, the toilet was located out in the tiny back yard that offered a spectacular view down over the city, almost all the way back to Togher far below.

On a sideboard in their living room, Uncle Bobby had an ageing PYE radio that, he reminded us each week, with renewed vehemence, was not to be touched. Worse than that, we were to stay a few feet away from it because the floor slanted and dipped at certain points and he was afraid we'd somehow bump up against the transistor (his name for it). He protected it so cautiously because he had two matches hammered into the dial so it was always tuned to what he called the BBC Light Programme, the frequency that delivered live sport every Wednesday and Saturday.

To step quickly or suddenly in the direction of the radio was to witness a man in complete control of his fast-twitch muscles. Uncle Bobby's reaction times when it came to intercepting one of us were those of somebody, we heard it whispered, 'had been a fine boxer in the Army'. Nobody told us which army but he moved with the panther-like grace of a featherweight rather than with the shuffle of the quiet, middle-aged man who earned his living making cars in the Ford factory down the Marina.

It was on Uncle Bobby's exalted radio one Saturday evening that I first heard the strains of an orchestra playing a march that went 'De dum, de dum, de dum, de dum, de diddly dum de dum.' A composition called 'Out of the Blue', it signified the start of BBC Radio's Sports Report at 5pm and the imminent arrival of James Alexander Gordon. He announced the classified football results in a wonderful voice whose inflections often gave away the identity of the winner before he'd finished the scoreline.

That first time I heard Gordon's memorable incantation, I watched Uncle Bobby listen intently as if under a spell, all the while diligently penciling every score into the empty slots next to each team's name in the fixture lists in the newspaper. From that point on, I became a devotee of this ceremony. I sat at our kitchen table at 5pm every Saturday, and waited for the distinctive march to start with my pen poised. Having recorded every result through the four English divisions and the Scottish Premier, I'd present my father with the handiwork for his perusal. He never failed to pretend to be impressed.

The house Uncle Bobby grew up in on Blarney Street had some curious attractions. Among them was a pile of old magazines that fascinated me. One stack was made up of *True Detectives*. The covers were grisly, risqué and sometimes scary, replete with sensational headlines ('The headless corpse in the Hollywood Hills!') and garish, bloody photographs. I wanted desperately to peek inside (what child wouldn't?) but I dared not. At least most of the time. Seeing how fastidiously he guarded his radio, I knew Uncle Bobby was not a man to be trifled with.

The second column was piled high with copies of *The Ring*, the bible of boxing. These we were allowed to read but only if we did so where he could see us and once we agreed to respect them at all times. No dog-earing pages. No rough treatment of his collection.

If he was in an especially benevolent mood and nobody had come within touching distance of his cherished radio, we might be allowed to take a couple home with us for a week. There was no signed contract involved in the loan arrangement, but there were many, many stipulations. I'm sure my father may have offered the car as collateral to guarantee their safe return more than once.

It was in this faded stack of American boxing literature dating back to the late 1960s that I got to read and re-read about Muhammad Ali, Joe Frazier and George Foreman. To open these pages was to enter a faraway world of pugilistic exotica. Aside from chronicling the golden era of the heavyweight division, they held reams of black and white photographs of boxers, most of whom we never heard about outside the pages of this august publication.

Then there were the advertisements. Every second ad seemed to offer some ingenious, newly discovered way to enhance physique and to improve muscle. Manna from heaven for a ten-year-old looking to bulk up so that he could one day turn pro on the soccer field. A constant source of torment for my father, especially when we were allowed bring *The Ring* home with us. As we waited on Adelaide Street, the meeting point to pick up my mother on the return journey, I passed the time trying to convince him to invest in my future.

'I'm reading about this thing called isokinetics – it's a new breakthrough in muscle building, and I want to…' I piped up from the backseat.

He never let me finish. 'It's a scam,' he said. 'All those ads are scams.'

As if that was going to put me off.

'What about the dyno-trainer?'

'The what?'

'The dyno-trainer. It has a built in flywheel rotor and double action for double the benefits.'

'You are making that up.'

'No, look at this guy,' I insisted, showing him the photograph of the muscle-bound behemoth accompanying the ad. He wasn't buying that either.

'That's a fake picture. Another scam.'

I was a sucker for these ads. This may have been because fitness, or at least finding a shortcut towards the increased strength that would give me an edge on the field, was something of an obsession of mine. *The Ring* wasn't the only source in that regard. Another publication was equally good in this regard. And this was one I could buy myself.

On Thursdays, I accompanied my mother to Dunnes Stores in Bishopstown where she bought the week's groceries. My reward for assisting her, long after my older siblings had grown out of the routine, was to be given the 18p or later 22p to buy *SHOOT!* magazine at the Read and Write newsagents a few doors down from the supermarket. On occasion, it was not delivered on time so I'd ask at the counter for it and some shop assistant might try to fob me off with last week's copy. The nerve. The ignorance. To think a devout anorak of a football fan could be so fooled.

Some people grow up in the thrall of great literature. Reared in houses lined with weighty bookshelves, they start thumbing through the classics from an early age and by the time they reach college, they can measure out their lives in the different literary phases: The Austen Years, The Hemingway Period, The Steinbeck Interlude, etc. Aside from my oldest sister Denise's well-thumbed copy of Thomas Hardy's *Tess of the d'Urbervilles*, we didn't have much of a library like that so I grew up reading *SHOOT!* religiously, from cover to cover. At least twice most weeks. It was a different type of education yet one that expanded my language, my horizons and, of course, my understanding of the beautiful game.

SHOOT! was where I learned words like 'perceptive', which was used to describe Liam Brady in a piece examining why Ireland constantly failed to qualify for major tournaments. Another favourite was 'fatigue', which was regularly trotted out to explain England's failure to perform even respectably at major tournaments. Another was 'consistent', which popped up in every bloody sentence mentioning the all-conquering Liverpool. Once I discovered a new and impressive word like this, I tried to work them into school essays so my teachers would think I was well-read and precocious.

I was neither. I was just devoted to *SHOOT!* to such an unhealthy degree that most of my knowledge of the wider world between 1978 and 1987 was gained through this very odd prism. This was where I first started to read about racism. When Bobby Robson announced an England squad that included six black players in October 1982, it was a seismic event in the history of the sport in Britain. I realised that much. But I would probably have benefited from a deeper perspective than the rather bizarre one I picked up in Phil Thompson's weekly column.

'They'll bring a new look to England, give us a touch of the old Brazilians' style,' wrote the Liverpool captain under the headline 'Boo Boys Boost Blacks'. 'If we can add a South American flavour to traditional English football then we can beat the world again…'

I'm not sure exactly how Ricky Hill (born in Paddington), Mark Chamberlain (Stoke on Trent), and Viv Anderson (Nottingham), were meant to infuse flair from a distant continent in another hemisphere that they'd never been to. But that was the least of the difficulties with Thompson's logic. The headline captured the very strangest part of his take on the whole business; he reckoned the racists had somehow helped these put-upon players make it to the top.

'Now that blacks are making the breakthrough into the international ranks I hope the racist fans will accept them and give them cheers instead of jeers,' he wrote. 'Although I haven't suffered as much as Ricky Hill and the rest, I know what it's like to be a target for the boo boys, to get an ear-lashing every time I've gone for the ball. Instead of putting me off my game, it's given me a boost. And that's been the case with these lads. The mockery has forced them into trying even harder – and their reward is a place in the England set-up. And I've a feeling they are here to stay. They won't let England down!'

The absurdity of Thompson's argument, comparing opposing fans taunting him because he embodied Liverpudlian dominance to the way black players were abused for the colour of their skin, went right over my childish head. It couldn't have done otherwise. This was a much less enlightened time where *Minder* was appointment television every Thursday night. In that show, it was considered fine for lovable rogue Arthur Daley to refer to a black character as a Lucozade, the derogatory Cockney rhyming slang for spade, or to call a gay man a poofter. The past was a different country. And not always a better one.

SHOOT! didn't stint from covering the major issues affecting society as a whole. It taught me the meaning of the word 'Thatcherism', something that hugely impressed my father. In a special report on falling attendances, the former Liverpool stalwart Emlyn Hughes lambasted Margaret Thatcher, blaming the dwindling gates in football on the fact too many supporters were now unemployed and unable to buy tickets for matches. From the other side of the political perspective, Manchester United's Gordon McQueen caused a brief flurry in the letters page after he called for professional footballers to pay lower taxes because of the relative brevity of their careers. Not a popular suggestion in a country wracked by strikes, lengthening dole queues and a growing economic divide between the haves and have-nots.

Befitting or perhaps reflecting such a turbulent time in society, this was also the dark age of hooliganism in the English game. Scarcely a week went by without an article or a letter in *SHOOT!* examining the causes, pondering the severity of the problem or offering solutions to the regular spectacle of yobs milling into each other inside and outside grounds. I recall England's goalkeeper Ray Clemence writing a piece with the headline 'The Day I Cried For My Country' about him feeling the full effects of the tear gas that Italian police sprayed at English fans during a game at the 1980 European Championships.

It was in these pages that I first came across the infamous photograph of a football fan with a dart in his eye on a terrace. A shocking sight to behold. The type of terrifying image that made me suddenly start to figure out that, no matter how entertaining and exciting the naïve child in me initially found the images of grown men fighting, this was really serious, genuinely horrific stuff. And not a combat spectacle to be savoured or joked about in any way.

SHOOT! aspired to lift the veil on the professional game, humanising our heroes by showing us them in real-life situations. An 'At Home with Gordon Hill' spread included a shot of the then Derby County winger, his wife Jackie and daughter Kerry all working hard ironing wrinkles from one of his England shirts. Probably something they did all the time.

There were other even more disturbing images. Andy Gray, during his stint as a regular contributor, once wrote a piece about his summer holidays, replete with photographs. They included him in his Speedos lounging around a beautiful swimming pool in a Los Angeles mansion owned by a member of Black Sabbath. I can't remember whether it was Geezer Butler's, Ozzy Osbourne's or Tony Iommi's house, but those images stayed with me for years afterwards. During my own subsequent, long-haired mullet flirtation with heavy metal in my mid-teens, I could never hear the opening riff of Sabbath's 'Paranoid' without picturing a nearly naked, gurning Gray.

Leeds United striker Frank Worthington was also captured in various domestic poses, his shirt opened to reveal luxuriant chest hair and medallion, with his new fiancée Carol Dwyer, declaring, 'It's the real thing this time!' It was an interesting montage showing the happy couple feeding a horse. As you do when you're in love.

Over the headline 'Brainy Bailey', Manchester United's Gary Bailey was pictured sitting at a computer console next to a mainframe that looked like it belonged on the set of *Buck Rogers in the 25th Century*. The perfect way to illustrate that he spent his spare time studying computer engineering at the city's Institute of Science and Technology.

There was no question then of players retiring to live off the money they earned. Wages were not what they are now. This much we knew because every edition carried a Q and

A called 'Focus On'. This was football's version of the Proust Questionnaire wherein the subjects revealed their innermost thoughts, or, at least, a succession of mundane details that offered clues about their lifestyles.

One query concerned the car they drove. The answers were reassuringly ordinary: Hillman Hunters, Volkswagen Jettas, Passats, Toyota Celicas and Corollas, Talbot Solaras, Ford Fiesta Supersports and Vauxhall Cavaliers. Most were just slightly souped-up versions of the vehicles driven by regular folk. It was kind of surprising that Mark Chamberlain, then an England international and father of the current Arsenal star Alex Oxlade-Chamberlain, didn't own a car at all.

In an era before diet and nutrition, the favourite meal question usually brought responses that included steak and chips, Dover sole and chicken tikka masala. The query about person they would most like to meet always seemed to be either Pelé or Muhammad Ali. George Benson and Luther Vandross featured regularly in the 'Favourite musician' slot although now and again somebody like QPR's Simon Stainrod might buck the trend by citing The B-52s and The Jam.

As eclectic as that might have seemed in the context of the professional game in that time, it was topped by Coventry City's Gerry Daly. The Republic of Ireland international answered that his favourite singers were Michael Jackson and Joe Dolan. Not sure how many of the fans in the English midlands understood the second half of that reference. Although he listed Pope John Paul II as the man he most wanted to meet, Daly also named the decidedly irreligious Benny Hill as his favourite actor.

Just in case the quiz hadn't been thorough enough, there was a section called 'Miscellaneous Likes and Dislikes'. The answers were never that thrilling 'Likes: situation comedies; Dislikes: injuries'. But, again, this expanded my lexicon. I can remember tormenting my father for a proper explanation and definition of the word 'miscellaneous' and, after growing increasingly exasperated, he declared, 'Don't worry about it. You'll never need to use that word!' He was right.

The real fun of the Focus On interview was imagining your own version of it. I regularly filled in my own answers to some of the questions.

Favourite Car: Morris Minor

Favourite Meal: Sausages, beans and chips

Favourite Singer: Adam and the Ants (assisted in this answer by sister Anne)

Favourite Country visited: Ireland (that was easy, I'd never been anywhere else)

Favourite TV Show: Minder (casual racism and all)

Favourite Holiday Resort: Garretstown

Toughest Opponent: My older brother

Biggest Disappointment: Not being taller

Biggest Influence on Career: My Dad

Person you would most like to meet: Pelé (well that's what everyone else put)

I was the type of impressionable young kid who had his head too easily turned by *SHOOT!*. I once read a Trevor Brooking interview in which he mentioned how dribbling a tennis ball to school helped him to improve his skills as a child. That was all I needed to know. I ferreted a balding Dunlop from the black hole that was our back garden shed and off I went the following morning. It was the least fun I've ever had kicking a ball and I almost got knocked down twice.

By the time I reached Mrs Applebee, the lollipop lady who patrolled the crossing at the bottom of the School Hill, I abandoned my efforts altogether. Disillusioned, I sat at my desk and concluded only that the streets of London, or wherever

Brooking grew up, must have been flatter than ours and not pockmarked by entrances to driveways. Either that or my first touch and control were woefully inadequate. I resolved to find other ways of improving myself and was soon devouring the 'Tricks of the Trade' column, a weekly feature designed to teach readers how to learn from the pros.

The art of dribbling was explained by then Ipswich Town and sometime Ireland winger Kevin O'Callaghan. His hardly ground-breaking advice involved putting six cones in a row and dribbling in and out of them at speed. Impressively conscious of the limited equipment available to children absorbing these instructions, O'Callaghan said jumpers could always be swapped for cones in emergencies.

'To dribble well, you must be able to keep the ball under control with both feet,' he wrote, sagely. 'Continue to do this until it comes almost natural to you.'

I did just as he said for weeks. It remained stubbornly unnatural to me. Obviously I just wasn't doing it right!

After splitting my sides at the 'Football Funnies', diligently answering the quizzes and filling in the crossword at speed, another staple of my reading diet was 'You are the Ref!' in which Clive Thomas, the greatest English official of the age, explained various conundrums that might occur during a match. They ranged from the straightforward:

Question: A player sent off in the first half comes to you during half-time and apologises. Should you accept this and allow him to play in the second half?

Answer: No! A player ordered from the field for misconduct cannot return.

…to the downright ridiculous:

Question: Can you take any action against a player who lights up a cigarette during a game?

Answer: Yes, the player should be cautioned for ungentlemanly conduct.

…to the obviously well-informed:

Question: Are goal-nets an essential requirement of the laws of the game?

Answer: No. Goal-nets are optional except in professional matches where they are a must. There are many times in junior matches where I have not been really sure whether a goal has been scored because there are no nets. I pity referees in these minor leagues.

In a time before Google existed, *SHOOT!* also offered 'Ask the Expert'. Readers were invited to write in with queries about football-related matters. An inquiry about whether, like Denis Law, any other famous players have represented Manchester United and Manchester City yielded an answer about Brian Kidd (who I'd heard of) and Billy Meredith (who I hadn't). This was where and how I learned the history of the game, about these icons from the past like Meredith, Alfredo di Stefano (played international football for Argentina, Colombia and Spain), and Nat Lofthouse (earned nickname of 'Lion of Vienna' following magnificent display against Austria in 1952).

When I had read and re-read every word of each issue, I then worked my way through the advertisements for soccer-related memorabilia and paraphernalia that cropped up on nearly every page. There were ads for absolutely everything in there, ads that I used to torment my mother about, imploring her to purchase the latest must-have accessory or to send me to 'One Touch Soccer Camp – the cure for the boring summer holiday.'

'Can I get this digital watch with Aston Villa on it?'

'No!'

'How about these Villa pyjamas? They are just £5.00 plus postage and packaging.'

'No!'

'Can I just show you this exclusive bomber jacket with Villa across the back shoulders?'

'No!'

'You have to see this. It's a Villa bedspread with the club crest and everything.'

'No!'

'Gary Shaw shin pads, just £2.20?

'No!!'

Towards the end of the 1970s, replica kits were starting to come on stream in a big way, although it's difficult to conceive of a factory outlet today admitting to readers, like Cash & Carry Sports of Surrey did, that it was selling England jerseys that were 'slight seconds'. At a time when most of the magazine was still black and white cheap paper, Admiral took out full-page ads in glossy colour showing Trevor Francis, Ray Wilkins and Glenn Hoddle modelling their distinctive kit with the red and blue blocks on the shoulders.

It was a time when footballers lent their name to strange products. Here's Kevin Keegan promoting a special commemorative medallion produced for Euro '80. There's Steve Coppell endorsing a series of publications by the Careers and Occupational Information Centre with racy titles like *Carpenter and Joiner, Driving Jobs–Road Transport* and *Professional Engineering and its Branches.*

'If your goal is a good job these books will help you score!' advised Coppell.

Arguably most bizarre of all were the ads for Bullworker. A German invention designed to improve strength, it was right up there with the fantastical fitness items I craved every time I opened the pages of *The Ring*. Except with one crucial difference. Peter Shilton endorsed Bullworker in *SHOOT!*.

Obviously, he was the best English goalkeeper of the time and one of the finest in the world but the topless photo of him accompanying the advertorial showed a man definitely and curiously bereft of the pneumatic pecs and jaw-dropping six-pack usually associated with flogging devices guaranteeing to help you bulk up.

It is a testament to my mother's shrewd budgeting, obstinacy and thrifty household management that she was resolute in refusing to listen to my eternal pleadings for the wide range of soccer products available. She never gave in. Never. Not once. She had more sense than money.

I tried my father a few times too and he took a different tack in the way he shot me down.

'They sell 8mm films of the greatest games every played and they are just £4.95!'

'The problem is we'd have to buy a projector first.'

'That's okay. They sell them too. Just £23.50.'

'Those are the cheap ones. They have a reputation for always breaking down. We'd be wasting our money.'

It was No. Just a different kind of No.

Sometimes, he'd try an even smarter tack.

'Why don't you save up every week and see how far you get?'

He knew that wasn't likely to happen. I had commitment issues.

After all, every August, *SHOOT!* came with sheaves of cardboard that were meant to allow you to cut out tabs and to keep your own league table every week. Your task was to place each club in their slot as per their position after the conclusion of the fixture list. This was supposed to be tremendous fun. The best part came before a ball was kicked. That's when I would put Aston Villa on top just to see what it looked like. And that was it. I never ever, ever touched it thereafter. By Christmas it was usually down behind my bed or buried beneath a mound of other football publications that I sourced from a different supplier.

Mrs Coffey's book shop stood a few doors up from the very bottom of Barrack Street, the southern access road to the medieval city, as my Dad relished telling me, just about every time I went there with him. A strange and wonderful place, halfway between a library and a store, it was governed by a unique commercial arrangement. When my father returned the books he'd bought there the previous week, the owner gave him back half what he paid. Then, he resumed the search for whatever he could find by Messrs Ludlum, Van Lustbader or Higgins. After making his own selections, he sought out a Catherine Cookson for my mother.

It was always at night when we went there and it was always cold. I know this because I remember Mrs Coffey, this genial old lady, inviting me behind the counter where a Superser heater, all three bars lit, was usually glowing. There, I'd sit on a stool, feeling the heat burning into my battleship-grey school uniform trousers. There, I'd answer a slew of questions about school and about books and about reading. Suitably satisfied that my commitment hadn't waned since last we spoke, she'd set me up with a pile of comics to sift through: *Tiger and Scorcher, Battle!, Roy of the Rovers, Warlord!, Hotspur* and *Commando*.

Of course, the militaristic publications didn't interest me as much as *Tiger* and *Roy of the Rovers*. It was a different buzz to the one afforded by *SHOOT!* but the footballing adventures of Roy Race, Billy Dane, Hotshot Hamish, Mighty Mouse, and

Gordon Stewart provided a hit too. The problem was I could get through one of their strips in a matter of minutes. *SHOOT!* offered a much more prolonged high. Not to mention my father was constantly telling me it was more educational.

Still, since Mrs Coffey was giving me free rein, I'd return home with a sample each week to spend time with these memorable characters. Hotshot Hamish, his Princes Park shirt struggling manfully to cover the lower half of his belly, and his long-range shots inevitably breaking the net. Mighty Mouse, the tubby, bespectacled doctor always running from an overnight shift at the hospital and an angry matron to a First Division game where he'd star for Tottenford Rovers. And, of course, Roy Race and his always dramatic exploits with Blackie Gray and the rest of the Melchester Rovers crew.

All of those held my interest but my two favourites featured the younger stars. In 'Tommy's Troubles', Tommy Barnes and his best friend, Ginger Collins, were soccer fanatics battling for the right to play the sport in a rugby-playing school. Their best efforts to promote the game and, eventually, to run their own team (Barnes United) were often scuppered by Waller and Swate, a bigger, stronger pair of oval-ball devotees and persistent bullies. For a working-class kid in Togher, the rugby stuff was puzzling because we had no exposure good or bad to that code. I didn't meet anybody remotely resembling Waller or Swate until I went to secondary school.

No matter. I enjoyed the travails of Barnes United. They played on fields as nondescript as those on which we cut our own footballing teeth. We had more than that in common too. They once took on a team of kids from Eastern Europe that utterly dominated them and eventually turned out to be robots. I regularly ran into opponents in the Cork Schoolboys' League who felt like they were made of iron and were hardwired to utterly decimate the likes of me.

'Billy's Boots' was another tale of a boy battling against the odds, relying on an ancient pair of boots with a supernatural connection to 'Deadshot Keene'. I wore a scapular around my neck that I kissed before games in order, my mother told me, to have the Lord on my side. We both believed in higher powers then, even if the mystical influence of a long-dead footballer seemed to yield much better and more immediate results for Billy. His boots were always moving him to just where he needed to be at precise moments in matches. No matter how many times I stood on the edge of the penalty box and waited for Jesus to guide me to where the ball was going to be, it never happened!

A metaphor, perhaps, for my entire career.

FOUR

A Stream Runs Through It

On Saturday mornings, my father rose first. As soon as I heard the tell-tale creak of the landing floor beneath his heavy feet, I was out of bed to follow him downstairs. I'd find him puttering about in the kitchen, filling the kettle, emptying the contents of the bread bin and fiddling with the toaster. Five days a week my mother made his breakfast and packed him a lunch before he left for work. At the weekend, he delivered a tray of tea and toast to her as she slept late. A lovely arrangement and a wonderful ritual, the true beauty of which only became apparent to me when I was much, much older.

As he did his domestic duty, a v-neck sweater hastily dragged over his sleeping vest so his unruly chest hair peeped out at various angles, I dressed myself, for I too had a part to play in the routine.

'Go get the paper,' he'd say, pressing coins into my hand.

It was my job to sprint (because before you are a teenager this is the only speed at which you are programmed to travel) across

Clashduv Road to the newsagent in nearby Riverview to get *The Cork Examiner*. Sometimes, if he was flush after a win on the horses, the order would include three Hamlet cigars and even a rather debonair instruction to keep the change on my return. Always, he took the paper, opened it onto the second page, then folded it in half and then half again so it was presented to my mother at the left-hand column announcing the deaths in the city and county. Her preferred breakfast included tea and lightly toasted brown bread with a healthy sliver of marmalade or jam scraped across it. And a swift and not at all morbid perusal of the news to see if anybody she knew had just died. Always she had a tone of strange disappointment when she didn't recognise any of the names listed.

There were definite perks to getting up early on Saturdays and Sundays. Having my father all to myself, however briefly, was one. Tapping him for easy money was another. And during one particularly bizarre series of events in the life of our street, there was one more.

On this particular Saturday in the spring of 1980, I completed my trip to the newsagent in record time, delivered the paper, wolfed down some burnt toast (during his solitary kitchen shift of the week it often took him more than one batch to get it just how she liked it) and then headed outside with a ball in my hand.

'I'm going to the square to play soccer,' I shouted already halfway towards the front door.

My father didn't even look up from the Jack Higgins novel he was already reading in his chair in the living room. Why would he have? This was my normal routine. Out into the empty square to kick the ball around until somebody/anybody woke up and joined me in my daily quest to prepare for an eventual life as a professional footballer. Except, I had something else in mind this time around than my chosen career. Sure, I juggled the ball going out the driveway for show, just in case my father turned his head and glanced out the window. After all, I didn't want to arouse any suspicion.

Upon reaching the square, I even went through the motions of embarking on a mazy dribble that ended with a deft side-foot finish into the goal or, more accurately, in between the black lines painted about ten feet apart along the iron bar fence that ran along one side of our playing area. The shot was only another ruse. My real interest was not honing the skills that one day would undoubtedly lead to me starring for Aston Villa and Ireland. I had more important business than soccer on hand as I jammed the ball into the space between the bars for safekeeping.

The moment it was secure, I set about my mission. I made for the nearby bridge, clambered up onto the stone balustrade and dismounted on the other side. Beneath me, the Glasheen Stream sauntered along at its usual stately pace. It had never looked quite so inviting.

Quickly, I skipped along the narrow verge of the right-hand bank, pulling some branches out of the way, like the intrepid explorer I also dreamed of one day being. Eventually, I found what I had been thinking about since the moment I woke up that morning, since the moment I put my head down to sleep the night before – a gleaming white bath tub. It nestled in the dense bushes and tangle of trees where the older boys, the ones who stayed out latest and used it last, had carefully stashed it away. For safekeeping.

When I reached it, I let out a 'Yes' and clenched my fist in triumph. I saw a paddle lying flat on the floor of the tub, another gift from the conscientious sailors who'd hauled her ashore the previous night. Another not quite so emphatic 'Yes'. Of course, when I say paddle, I mean the ancient hurley, replete with rusty splice, that had been liberated from someone's shed and pressganged into service on the high seas.

Four days before, the bath tub had come into our lives and changed them forever. Well, for a couple of weeks at least. Its exact provenance was unknown or perhaps initially just kept from us younger kids. The older brothers naturally regarded us as potential security breaches with our big mouths. They knew we'd crack under the slightest parental questioning so they often decided ignorance was the best policy. At least for as long as they could keep schtum and stop themselves from boasting about their latest feat of derring-do.

'It came from one of the new housing estates out by the church,' confided Tom from the bottom bunk a couple of nights earlier. He couldn't resist the brag because he knew that even that sliver of information was thrilling enough to set me off.

A group of them had travelled by foot a couple of miles from our street, gone past the Church of the Way of the Cross and out to where farmland was being turned at great speed into rows upon rows of new houses. These intrepid characters had found/discovered/stolen the tub and then carried it the same distance back to Clashduv. Aside from being quite the feat of strength and endurance, this involved walking along a couple of the busiest roads in Togher, nay, all of Cork.

At every point in that return journey, they were at great risk. Yet, extraordinarily, this gaggle of kids who had freed a bath tub from a half-finished house were able to ferry their prize a couple of miles along packed thoroughfares while nobody batted an eyelid. No beat cop walked or drove by and thought it somewhat unusual. No parents happened upon the scene and found it slightly troubling. No, just some likely lads carrying a bath tub down the street, a four-`man team of miniature movers transporting an essential bathroom fixture.

Later, the heroes involved confessed to stopping for breaks every fifty yards or so, carefully laying the fibreglass construct on the ground for fear of cracking the hull. No point going to all that trouble and having the vessel not be sea-worthy.

Our house abutted a block of flats and I was on the second-floor balcony next door when I saw them arriving back with their prize. I saw them straggling along the road, buckling under the strain of the great effort to bring home the biggest trophy any of us had ever seen. They reached the bridge and only paused briefly. They were too excited now that the journey was near the end. They worked together to hoist it over, like child actors on a 'Sesame Street' sketch about co-operation.

By then I had sprinted downstairs for a closer view. So too had several other urchins wondering what strange enterprise was afoot.

Once they had the tub over the wall, they lowered it towards the water, this quartet of adolescent Harland and Wolff cranes guiding one more boat into its natural habitat. Within minutes, the hurley having been purloined from some place with impressive speed, they were sailing up and down stream like old hands, shouting things like 'Ship Ahoy' and invoking the name of Captain Birdseye. I watched through the bars, shouting my approval and begging to have my ticket punched so I too might set sail in this brave new world.

Eventually, I got the nod and was standing by the riverbank where, with typical diligence and ingenuity, the older boys had already started to hack away at the vegetation to create a space from which the passengers could embark and disembark. Tom was the captain for *my* maiden voyage, and he barked one rule at me. 'Don't move once you sit in.'

I didn't. I dared not.

I was just too happy to be there, alongside him, afloat, to risk messing it up. Too excited to be glimpsing this river that had been a feature of all our lives from this whole new angle. He brushed the boat against the side of the bank, not sure if that was by accident or designed to spook me. Then he took me towards the edge of the darkness where the river disappeared into the gloom of the bridge that ran across Clashduv Road. Then he did a class of a trick with the hurley that made the tub turn fast in the water. He was definitely showing off but I didn't speak lest I annoy him. I was too intoxicated by the thrill of the new, the prospect of how much fun we could knock out of this marvellous addition to our lives.

That first cruise was brief yet memorable enough that I, of course, wanted more. The problem was so did everybody else. For now we all shelved our plans to be the next Kevin Keegan or Jimmy Barry-Murphy. These were mundane enough heroes compared to Christopher Columbus. We wanted to explore uncharted territory or at least pluck up the courage to take the tub through the darkness, beneath Clashduv Road, and all the way to the other side of the bridge.

The arrival of the bath tub that thought itself a yacht caused an outbreak of nautical excitement in the dry docks of our lives. The problem with something as wonderful as an improvised boat sailing on a river in a concrete and tarmacadam suburb where most kids saw the beach once a year (if they were lucky) was that word got around quickly. Togher's bush telegraph thrummed with the news of this great novelty. Kids we barely knew started to arrive in droves from other streets. Interlopers from Maple Place. Hijackers from Whitebeam Road. Bloody tourists from up by the Five Star shopping centre.

Everybody wanted a go and, although there were a few fights about queue-jumping, most of them hung around patiently each day until a space opened up and they could clamber in for the trip of a lifetime. A grandiloquent phrase to describe a journey of perhaps twenty yards in total but one that accurately captured our joy at being afloat, moving on water, however slowly, however briefly.

This boat/domestic washing facility had been in such high demand since its first appearance that getting any quality time aboard proved more and more difficult as the days went by. Not to mention the chances of a solo voyage were nearly impossible altogether. So, this is why I spent the whole week plotting, and happened upon my rather ingenious scheme to arrive on Saturday at the earliest possible time.

My plan was very simple: get there before the others had even stirred from their beds. And it was proceeding perfectly. I planted my feet in the mud just inches from the water and I started to haul the tub down towards it. It looked lighter when I'd seen my brother and other bigger kids do it. But I heaved and heaved and it started to move. Then I leapt out of the way as it slid into the water. I was careful to keep one hand holding the side lest it drift off. Leaning over to pick up the hurley with the other hand, I jumped in. With a little too much enthusiasm. The tub leaned treacherously to one side until I shifted my bum and righted the ship.

This was it. At last. I was master of my own destiny, I pushed away from the bank. My boat and I. My *Niña*, my *Pinta*, my *Santa Maria*. I took a deep breath and leaned against the back of the tub like a man taking a bath after a hard day's labour. Slowly I paddled towards the darkness where the stream disappeared beneath the bridge. I heard the cars trundling by overhead. I could, with some difficulty, see the rectangle of light in the distance where the stream returned to open land on the other side. And that's where I, come hell or high water, was determined to go…

When I was born in January 1971, we were living in a bungalow on Plunkett Road in Ballyphehane. My arrival was, I later discovered, unplanned and unexpected, but provided one unlikely boon. Crucially, a fourth child bumped the family up the Cork Corporation housing list and so, a year after I came on the scene, we were given the keys to a freshly built three-bedroomed house, a mile to the west in the neighbouring suburb of Togher. Obviously, I don't remember much about this event but was fascinated to learn the detail that all our worldly possessions were transported to our new home using bicycles and prams. My father had not yet saved up to buy his first Morris Minor.

A couple of thousand other families arrived in Togher around that time in similar circumstances, beneficiaries of the government's new determination to try to provide proper modern public housing to those who needed it around the country. As a result, what was once a charming rural village on the outskirts of the city was then in the process of being quickly subsumed into the relentless urban sprawl. A steady stream of new houses and flats went up every year, which meant hundreds more kids were teeming the streets. And oh so little town planning in the midst of it all.

Nobody in a position of authority appears to have thought it might be useful to punctuate the rows of functional two- and three-storey constructions with proper recreational facilities such as parks and playgrounds. As if anybody would need or benefit from these sort of superfluities in a swatch of territory where every house boasted a hive of growing children. Not to mention too that this was in an age when parents believed kids should be out of the house whenever the weather allowed – for as long as possible.

The absence of basic facilities was later inevitably and justifiably blamed when Togher started to suffer its share of what are euphemistically called 'social problems'. In its own perverse way, though, the lack was a kind of gift to us. We were forced to lean upon our own ingenuity in the eternal quest for fun. Like the hunter-gatherers of the Paleolithic age, we adapted to the situation, learning quickly to exploit everything and anything that we found in the world around us. We turned each available space into an opportunity or a place for play. In this respect our richest resource by far was the Glasheen Stream.

A body of water that meandered along twenty yards from our front door, it was caged behind rows of six-foot-high iron bars as if it was some wild beast that needed to be tamed. In reality, it was a babbling brook that sometimes resembled an open sewer, but in our childish imaginations was always and forever a real river. Huck Finn had the broad majesty of the Mississippi, we had the more diminutive epic that was the Glasheen Stream.

The water was never more than two feet deep, only really swelling to that depth after torrential rain of a type that also turned it a nasty shade of brown, resembling sewage. Otherwise, it trickled along in a manner which lived up to its original medieval Irish name, Glaisín na Shearnaighe, the murmuring river.

If it was a stream that we thought was a river and imagined to be an ocean, it was also unlike just about any other body of water I've encountered since. For starters, none of us ever saw a fish or an aquatic creature worthy of the name in among the abandoned bikes and shopping trolleys that often found a home there. I don't even recall a lurking frog in or around it. Thinking back, this may have been a fair indicator that the stream's use as a dumping ground for waste during the Industrial Revolution in nearby Glasheen a century before must have purged it of all living organisms. Except one especially resilient species: the rat.

The first time I saw a rat scuttle along the bank while we moseyed just feet away, I barely flinched. I was six so we can call it the fearlessness of youth. Or, maybe, the ignorance of a child to the danger posed. Perhaps, I was already programmed not to show any weakness in front of the older kids, especially Tom. I had learned fairly sharpish that if him and his pals didn't display any fear of something, then neither would I. The youngest always does what he must to gain the acceptance he craves.

Still, the rats were dark brown, menacing beasts. We sometimes sat on the bridge across the river and watched them scurry out of a series of open pipes that protruded from the river bank. Careful, stealthy creatures, they'd pause at the edge of the pipe, look around and then make their move into the open. In our youthful folly, we talked a lot more about where the rats were going and coming from than we ever did about the pipes. Just what were they leaking into the river? And where did the pipes even originate? These were not questions that ever seriously bothered us. Or anybody in authority who probably should have been making discreet enquiries.

Perhaps because of the thriving colony of rats that lived there, our mothers frowned upon our use of the Glasheen Stream for recreation. As was customary in 1970s and 1980s Ireland, their warnings to stay out of the place came laced with the usual apocalyptic fervour. 'You'll catch Yellow Fever out of that place there!' was my own mam's favourite admonition. It was delivered with genuine passion as if the chances of me contracting the disease were actually huge.

Her concerns fell on deaf ears because Yellow Fever just wasn't realistic enough a threat to my well-being. I never heard of anybody at school missing a few days with Yellow Fever. I'd never seen any of my extended family struck down with Yellow Fever, and I overheard my mother talk about every illness known to man – even the dreaded rickets!

I didn't quite understand why then this was the main disease she felt we would contract from the admittedly less than clean stream we had converted into our very own waterpark. There weren't even that many mosquitos flitting around the stream to transmit the virus – again, in itself, one more telling detail offering clues to how rancid the place must actually have been.

I like to think now that my mother had an especially long folk memory and remembered the damage Yellow Fever wrought in Ireland back in the 1820s. But I really have no idea why this was her ailment of choice to try to frighten us into staying landlubbers forever.

At one point I was so frustrated with her banning us from the stream that I spent part of an evening pretending to do homework but really looking up Yellow Fever in the *Student's Merit Encyclopedia*. These were twenty-six faux-leather volumes that took up the long shelf in the cabinet by my father's chair. He constantly assured me that they 'contained everything you ever needed to know in the world'. I think he liked to say that out loud to justify the fact my parents had bought them on a hire purchase scheme that took years to pay off, years in which those tomes largely gathered dust.

In any case, it was in one of those books that I discovered Yellow Fever was by that point in the late twentieth century largely restricted to Africa and South America. Not a word in there about Ireland or even our neighbours in England suffering the odd outbreak. I also learned the symptoms were fever, chills, loss of appetite and nausea. I occasionally left the stream sweating, but never chilly and always ravenously hungry. The latter may have been because according to a government regulation adhered to strictly by all Togher mothers there was no snacking between meals. This may also explain why we gobbled everything put in front of us when we did finally sit down.

We ignored all public health warnings issued by the maternal authorities (the fathers were either at work or hadn't been keeping up to date with the various medical epidemics threatening their kids). We had to because the stream was too much fun. Sometimes, we went there just to sit in the trees and do nothing. Unless somebody was in possession of a Swiss Army Knife. Then we'd carve our initials and the date into the bark so that future generations could timestamp our contribution to civilization. These were our cave paintings, the artistic high water mark of a thriving urban society.

When we grew tired of our own stretch of the stream, we went exploring its length and breadth. This involved hacking our way through overgrowth like great explorers then peeking over walls into the private houses that backed onto it upriver. Over time we grew to know which ones had apple trees that would be ripe for the picking in autumn. Having checked for dogs, we bounded into those gardens and filled our jumpers with as many apples as we could muster while still being able to get back up over the wall. The more enterprising petty thieves among us brought plastic bags. These were usually also the cheeky boys who waved back if an angry homeowner rapped upon a back window to warn us to stop. On those occasions when I saw a red-faced resident had rumbled us, I abandoned all apples and scurried for the wall.

Upon returning to our own patch with our ill-gotten bounty, we sat there munching happily until our stomachs hurt. Then we started firing the spare apples at other kids walking along Clashduv Road, always making sure to only aim for those smaller than us. We weren't idiots after all. Actually, strike that, some of us were. At least one of our number usually walked home either juggling apples, dribbling them like soccer balls or eating one in each hand like some sort of fruit-eating big shot. If my mother saw this, and she did love looking out the front window, the normal prohibitions about the stream then became skewed.

'Were ye slogging down the stream?' she asked, using the preferred slang term for the act of invading somebody's property to steal from their trees.

'No,' I replied, not sure of her mood.

'Are you sure?'

'Eh.'

'Have ye any left?'

'There's a stash over by the stream.'

'Go get them and I'll make ye an apple tart,' she said, her eyes rolling to signify, yes, this was a breach of the rules but one that might benefit us all.

From time to time, someone procured a rope and a piece of timber was quickly attached to the end so that we fashioned a swing to dangle from the highest branch of one of the sturdier trees. For a kid who loved watching the black and white *Tarzan* movies with my father, this was not just a thrill, this was a chance to go full Johnny Weissmuller. 'Awawawaw!!!' I bellowed, doing my best attempt to mimic the ululating yell he used to call the animals of the jungle in a time of crisis.

If being airborne out over the water felt magnificent, it got old after a while so we'd search for ways to wring new kicks from this contraption. This usually culminated in us trying to see how many boys could hold on to the rope at any given time. Four or five of us clambered aboard in mid-swing, clutching at a sliver of available rope, shrieking excitedly before, inevitably, almost theatrically, the swing snapped and every passenger ended up falling from a height to be soaked in water and caked in mud.

The coldness of that drenching was as nothing compared to the frosty reception that awaited us when we trudged home in that condition to show our mothers what our fun and games had done to our clothes. Every maternal explosion in those instances involved a soliloquy about laundry and was bookended by the wistful declaration 'And you know there's no drying in this weather!' In a time before washer-dryers, this was a generation who spent large parts of each day obsessing over the ability to hang wet clothes on the lines that latticed the airspace above every back garden.

Occasionally, a vigilant mother might look out her window and through the trees spy a child of hers in the stream from which he was banned. That's when the real fun would start. Suddenly, she'd appear on the bridge, roaring his name and demanding he leave forthwith. If we were lucky, the show might lead to him getting a few smacks upside the head as he was dragged home. We laughed at his misfortune, knowing he would laugh at ours when our turn came. And it would come. Our commitment to the stream ensured the wrath of the angry mother came to us all eventually. It was just one of the perils of the job. All who explored the stream did so knowing the risks involved.

Still, nothing they could say or do kept us away from the stream because it had too much to offer. Every June, we'd climb over the bridge carrying all manner of sharp objects and commit egregious crimes against nature. My weapon of choice was a heavy iron meat cleaver that one of my uncles had, ahem, borrowed from Lunham's Meat Factory and, conveniently for me, left in our shed.

The sight of a child, a veritable boy soldier, clutching a weapon capable of slicing through cow carcasses never attracted any attention from passers-by. How could it have? They were probably too busy staring at Ian O'Leary with an axe in his hand or Barry Geoghegan cradling some especially lethal-looking saw with serrated teeth destined to make short work of any tree trunk.

And, of course, that's what we were there to do. In the weeks building up to Bonfire Night, we rambled the banks of the stream chopping down perfectly good trees, so many hard-working and resourceful lumberjacks. We did not discriminate. An old willow that reeked of history or a recently planted sapling still bearing the handprints of the Cork Corporation workers who put it there as some sort of spruce-the-place-up initiative, we didn't mind. We hacked them all down.

If we could reach it we could cut it and place it on the pyre that we held in honour of we knew not what each 23 June. That nobody really understood St John's Eve was the reason for the annual fire on that particular date scarcely mattered when it gave us an excuse to play with matches on a grand scale. And all boys and a lot of girls love starting fires and watching them blaze.

Years before global warming and the ozone layer became part of our education, we were wrecking crews sent to speed up the death of the planet. We performed our task with gusto. Older boys did the cutting of the branches. Younger kids dragged the prematurely murdered trees out over the bridge to the nearby bog where the fire was traditionally located.

Nobody ever prevented us or asked us to stop or pointed out the folly of what we were at. Never. Not once. Ever. By the 1980s, young people all over the planet were styling themselves as eco-warriors fighting to conserve and preserve nature's bounty. We were the opposite. Every June we took it upon ourselves to embark on some impromptu deforestation of all trees native to the Glasheen Stream. Years later, we saw Sting holding a press conference alongside the chief of a tribe from the Amazon rainforest and learned all about the importance of trees to the health of the earth. By which time it was a little late.

As the bath tub edged forward and into the darkness under the bridge, I started to regret my decision to embark on a solo voyage. Sure, I could see the light on the other side, but the deeper I went into the gloom the farther away the brightness seemed to be. Every time I pushed the hurley down into the water, I feared pushing against a rat out for his morning constitutional. I deliberately steered a path down the centre of the water because I'd heard older boys say that the rats mainly swam along the side. I was never sure about the truth of that.

Strangely enough, the deeper into the Stygian murk I ventured the calmer I became. I could do this. Older lads had been doing it all week. Back and forth. No problem. So I paddled and I kept as still as I could. At one point, I felt rocks scraping against the hull and put my hands underneath my legs to see if any water was coming through in a Titanic-type situation. It wasn't. On I went.

The cars and trucks flying by on the road just inches above my head provided an unsettling soundtrack to my journey. Every now and again, an articulated lorry would make the bridge shake and rattle and the noise made me to start to wonder how long it might take for them to find my pancaked body if the thing collapsed. Eventually, my positive thinking was rewarded. The light came closer. The hurley did the paddling job it was never designed to do. Finally, I pushed forward and emerged into daylight. I had reached the other side.

I lifted the hurley out of the water and raised it above my head in triumph. I was Stanley finally tracking down Livingstone in Africa. I was Lewis and Clark charting a path to the Pacific Ocean. I was nine years old and I had sailed fifty feet along a dark underground river in a bath tub.

FIVE

Wide World of Sport

On 10 September 1966 Donogh O'Malley, then Minister for Education, made a speech lamenting the fact that every year 17,000 Irish boys and girls were unable to move on from primary to secondary school because their families could not afford the fees involved. O'Malley was determined to change that. He wanted free post-primary education to be available as a right to every child, regardless of their economic circumstances. The subsequent legislation on education changed the fortunes of my family and so many others forever.

My sister Denise, the oldest child, was a few months short of her second birthday when O'Malley unveiled his ambitious scheme. Just over a decade later, she enrolled in St Aloysius Girls' School on Sharman Crawford Street. One small step for her, one giant step for my parents because she was going further into education than either of them ever did. They were one of the previous generations deprived of opportunities that lay tantalisingly beyond their families' means. They were the very kind of people whose plight O'Malley had realised was a blight on the whole nation.

As the eldest of eleven kids, my mother started full-time work at twelve and, like many of her female peers in the city, eventually got a job working in the Sunbeam clothes factory in Blackpool. One of eight children, my father's career followed a similar path and, by his late teens, he was shoveling coal in the engine room of a train on the old Cork-Bandon rail line. He delighted in reminding us of this every time we watched one of those old western movies when bandits were inevitably lying in wait down the tracks, bent on holding up the train.

'They never tried that when I was on duty!'

To my parents then, given the reality they had endured at a similar age, the sight of their eldest daughter putting on the dark green uniform and readying herself to head off to secondary school was a source of unimaginable pride. Which explains why my mother spent months ensuring she had everything she required for this new phase of her life.

Among the litany of requirements for starting at the new school, Denise was, apparently, required to get a tennis racquet. I'm not sure if this was actually an official demand or whether she merely convinced my parents that it was an aspirational necessity. It didn't matter either way. They were so exultant about her impending enrolment that if she had asked for a spaceship to get to school, my father might have put in an exploratory phone call to NASA just to see if they had any available second-hand rockets they were looking to offload at a reasonable price.

This was how the first real tennis racquet – from Matthews' sports shop in town no less – came into the Hannigan household. It wasn't any of the brands we later understood to be the market leaders in the sport but it was far removed from the disposable productions we usually employed. We knew it was of a certain quality because of the hardness of the strings and how taut they were. When I banged it off my head that first day it hurt a lot. Which didn't stop me continuing to road-test it against my noggin every time I picked it up to play. As I matured I figured out serious tennis players used the butt of the palm of their hand to test the tension of the strings.

When Denise saw me manhandling it that first day, she took the racquet off me and warned us all that it was off-limits forever. The sort of prohibition that made us all the more determined to get our hands on it whenever her back was turned. There was no great need for subterfuge in any case. Sometime in first year, her promising tennis career and her dreams of becoming the next Chris Evert derailed. Luckily for her younger brothers, she lost interest in the game and we gained a serious tennis racquet. This was essential for the fortnight every July that we watched Wimbledon and were duly inspired to try to serve aces and whip passing shots down baselines that were often imaginary or, at best, etched haphazardly in chalk.

That we were so motivated and driven to emulate Björn Borg is all the more remarkable given that there wasn't a tennis court for miles. At least not one that we were allowed in to. We didn't need facilities like the All-England club though, we had the square around which our houses had been built. It was flat and, because this was the late 1970s and early '80s, it hadn't yet filled up with parked cars. We had a large tract of flat concrete then and we drew the lines of a court with the fastidiousness of officials of the All-England club.

In the interests of verisimilitude, we went as far as scratching out the doubles lines even though we were a community that only ever really played singles matches. Still, looks were important. In these encounters, the Hannigan boys had an in-built advantage. We were swinging our sister's serious racquet. The ball sprung from it with much greater force than those inferior weapons being wielded by our opponents, disposable versions that had been purchased in Youghal or Kinsale during a day at the seaside.

This was not a level playing field.

Later, we added to our arsenal when an early prototype of the aluminium racquets found its way into our possession, gifted to us by one of our uncles. This wasn't quite as potent but it did greatly resemble the one used by Jimmy Connors. The style points gained from that made it worth suffering a sting to the hands every time I hit the ball anywhere except the dead centre of the strings – which was about nine times out of ten.

Occasionally, just to torture ourselves, we visited the racquet section at Johnny Giles' Sports after it opened to feel the strings of the truly expensive models, gasping as much at the prices as we did at how perfectly they sounded when we swung them at imaginary balls as the shop assistants watched on nervously. If one of us had money, we eventually sidled up to the counter with a three-pack of yellow balls, acting like we were off to grace the manicured grass of Sunday's Well tennis club, not returning to the asphalt centre-court of Clashduv Road.

On the really committed days, when Borg or John McEnroe had set fire to our imaginations, we would go to extraordinary lengths to replicate their feats. Kitchen chairs were liberated from houses, snaffled through the back doors and taken out the side gates as mothers were otherwise engaged. String or rope was found somewhere to stretch between the two chairs and voila, we had a net. Well sort of.

It was at least a guideline showing where the ball was supposed to go over. Inevitably, sometimes, the ball went too fast and we couldn't tell whether it went over or under and that's when the trouble started. The children of Clashduv Road could have avoided a world of hurt and more than one outbreak of violent fisticuffs if Hawk-Eye technology had been available back then.

Most of the time, we eschewed the net completely, which meant our version of tennis was slightly different than the one we watched devoutly for, oh, all of two weeks each year. For starters, we never understood how the professionals so often hit the net with their first serve. In the absence of any net, this was never an issue for us. Our game involved trying to land the ball just over the squiggeldy chalk line. Our rallies didn't last long either. How could they have? All you had to do was swipe the ball low along the ground, just enough to cross the line, and it was almost impossible to return.

I was maybe seven when Tom brought the chess bug into the house. Like everybody else who passed through Mr Healy's fifth class, he learned to play and then, for a time, couldn't stop. Even better, though, he took the time out to teach me the rudiments of the game. That was a tough gig as I struggled, in particular, to understand the powers of the knight. Castling was another move that perplexed me.

I often wondered why he went to such trouble, putting in all that effort to help me. Many years later, it hit me. He needed an opponent and there's nothing better than playing somebody you can defeat easily every time. I must have done wonders for his confidence and he was soon on the school team.

As with everything else Tom ever did, good and bad, I immediately aspired to emulating him. I could only learn so much from his ritualistic daily beat-downs of me so I went looking for extra help. My father never played and, perhaps worried he'd have to play me every night, declared himself too old to learn. But, as usual, he was anxious to encourage my interest in whatever way he could.

One night, he returned from work carrying a small white paperback called *Begin Chess* by DB Pritchard. He never explained its origins, just that he'd seen it in one of the second-hand book shops he liked to frequent. I didn't care where it came from. I just appreciated the gift. I was a neophyte taking possession of his first bible. Within the year, the cover, a sketch of a boy around my age intently studying his position with his hand on his forehead, started to fray from constant use. The spine became stretched as I kept the book open so I could copy openings and endings from within its pages.

The struggle for children with chess is not mastering the intricacies of the Sicilian Defence or the Queen's Gambit but the constant battle not to lose pieces. Often a toy soldier or even a penny might have to be pressed into service in the stead of a missing pawn or rook. The presence of a substitute seriously detracted from the look of the board but didn't diminish our enjoyment any. I was hooked.

Soon, my father alerted me to the *Evening Echo*'s weekly chess column chronicling the exploits of burgeoning city legends like Mel Kennedy and Philip Short. The accounts of local competitions didn't interest me as much as the conundrum that was posed at the bottom. I spent more time trying to figure that out than I ever devoted to homework.

For a while, the obsession was such that we got a travel chess set so we could play in the car. A miniature affair where the pawns were so impossibly thin they were difficult to grip. It didn't matter. We just wanted to play. A magnetic chess set was next up, the pieces sliding along the surface of the board and, miraculously, sticking to it even when held upside down. Imagine the excitement the first hundred times we did that and they stayed in place.

We went through a succession of cheap chess sets too. I know they were cheap because of how easily the plastic figures smashed when they fell on the kitchen floor. This was almost certainly a flaw in the manufacturing, an indication of poor quality materials or, as my mother pointed out, a reflection of how hard an irate child threw them when miffed at squandering a winning position and losing to his older brother. Again.

Tom stopped playing after leaving primary school but by then I had daily competitions with the other kids in my class who, like me, aspired to one day making the school team. The make-up of the A and B squads, including a travelling sub, was decided by a fiercely-contested in-house tournament that dragged on for weeks. To be involved often meant getting special treatment. A match that began during lunch hour and didn't conclude in the time available might be allowed to continue at the back of the classroom. The teachers had no choice but to extend this privilege. They were under pressure to come up with the line-ups ahead of the opening clashes with other schools.

Once you made the team the real fun began. We travelled all over the city, arriving into empty buildings where one classroom was set up exclusively for chess. There we pitted our wits and furrowed our brows against similarly earnest kids from Scoil Chríost Rí or the North Monastery or Togher BNS. I remember all these schools smelled exactly like our own and each was attended at that time of the day by the same eerie quiet of departed children.

My finest moment as a school chess player was eking out a draw from a dreadful losing position up in Greenmount BNS. The longer I dragged the contest out, the more frustrated my opponent was getting, an emotion no doubt shared by everybody else waiting for us to finish so they could go home. At one point during that marathon, I mentioned the fifty-move rule where a draw can be declared if neither player has made a capture in that time frame. There was some debate then between the teachers about whether this could be used. Of course, at that juncture I invoked DB Pritchard.

'I read about it in *Begin Chess*!'

In the end, possibly because everybody else in the room was desperate to go home, I snagged my half-point!

The only other adult in our family who was interested in chess was my uncle Noel. Married to my Aunty Phil, Noel was a bearded bricklayer by trade. He invited me to join him on Friday night pilgrimages to the CCYMS hall on Castle Street in the centre of town. There, we went upstairs into a room where a dozen or so other knights of the board gathered each week. A chess club that felt more like a clandestine gathering, the meeting of some secret society. All we were short was a dodgy handshake.

On the footpaths below, the city centre was starting to thrum with the sound of weekend revelers. Behind those doors, however, we were oblivious to that tawdry spectacle, too busy obsessing over the loss of a pawn or the failure of a gambit. School matches were tremendous adventures, as much about the journey as the game itself, but the CCYMS felt different. This was a far more professional milieu.

There were people in that room using actual chess clocks, taking the care to write down every move made. I'd only ever seen that done on television. Conversations might be going on between tables about postal chess. I'd heard of it. I'd read about it. These grandmasters (that's what all of them were to me) were actually doing it. I don't think I ever won a game on any of those Friday nights but I loved the ritual because, for a couple of years, I loved the game so much. Until, just like with my brother before me, the affair ended abruptly and inexplicably when I started secondary school.

Our thirst for sport was unquenchable and often bizarrely wedded to the calendar. Every first week of August, for instance, we sat in front of the television and watched RTÉ's live coverage of the showjumping from the RDS in Dublin. From start to finish. Now, most of us, to my knowledge, had never seen or touched a live horse, been in the vicinity of a stable or had any experience of anything to do with the equine world – aside, of course, from our father's squandering money at the bookie's on ill-fated nags that never won. Yet we were captivated by our annual glimpse of this peculiar demi-monde. We actually, genuinely, seriously cared about who won the Aga Khan Trophy.

We had no idea this impressive bauble was named for the man who donated it decades before Sir Sultan Muhammad Shad or Aga Khan III, an Imam from what was then British India but is now known as Pakistan. We merely knew that it was live sport, there was an Irish team competing and one with a real chance of winning (not a regular occurrence in most sports those days). An Irish team too that we could cheer on from our living rooms. So we did.

For a few years this was a fixture during our summer holidays as we briefly lived and died with the performances of Paul Darragh, Captain Con Power, James Kiernan, and, every arriviste fan's favourite, Eddie Macken on his faithful steed Boomerang.

In 1979, the edition that possibly hooked us all, Ireland was poised to make history. Any country that won the Aga Khan three times in a row got to take possession of the trophy forever. This Irish quartet was coming off the back of two consecutive victories so the pressure was on. It all came down to Captain Con Power on Rockbarton. Here was something none of us had ever seen live before, an Irish soldier in full military regalia representing the nation in battle against dastardly foreign powers.

As a spectacle, it was all very different to what we were used to. The riders went around the arena in near silence, a quiet so eerie that you sometimes heard a child crying in the background as the adults watched with bated breath. When Power rattled one of the bars on a jump at the halfway point of his ride into history, there was an audible gasp. The etiquette was all strangely polite compared to what we were used to in our own sports. When he knocked the top part of the middle fence at the subsequent combination, the crowd released a collective gasp. No swearing. Not an f-bomb was dropped apart from perhaps in a certain living room in Togher, many, many miles from the action.

Power was officer material for a reason. He recovered his composure and, with a cushion that meant he could afford to knock one fence, rode flawlessly the rest of the way to bring the trophy home. Ireland had won. Again. We were on our feet in Clashduv Road. Arms in the air. Like it really, really mattered.

I had never seen a saddle or a stirrup and didn't conceive of a way that I'd ever come near them either. My only experience of horse riding was virtual. Our day trips to Kinsale or Crosshaven on summer afternoons always culminated in a trip to the 'The Merries', the temporary amusement parks where our parents paid money so we could clamber up on sculpted horses and ride a carousel that moved just faster than walking pace. No matter how hard you urged those stallions on, they never quickened any.

If this was not a sport we were ever aspiring to participate in, it's all the more remarkable that the unavailability and the distance from our reality didn't diminish our enthusiasm. We celebrated this victory and others with gusto. I guess the best theory that explains why is that here was an Irish team excelling at something on the world stage. The 1980s eventually yielded Barry McGuigan, Stephen Roche, the Charlton Years, and, if you were into it, rugby Triple Crowns. But the 1970s were grim. Ireland never did well at anything. Really. Except showjumping. Indeed we became so immersed in the whole culture that we savoured the tabloid photographs of the English rider Harvey Smith, giving two fingers to somebody or other.

And, of course, we figured out a way to improvise our own version of the Aga Khan. For this, we convened in the O'Learys' back garden. It was long and flat and the grass was always neatly shorn. Perfect for what we had in store. Not only that, their shed was also piled high with paint tins of all shapes and sizes. Once we sourced enough timber slats and a couple of hurleys, we had the materials to start building fences and a proper course. Test runs were even carried out to make sure there was enough space in between the jumps.

Like every other contest on the street, the staging of the event was always attended by strange arguments. There might be a complaint about the lack of a water jump and speculation about how Mr and Mrs O'Leary might react if we dug a hole in their lawn and filled it. We never tested their resolve on that score. Then a discussion could ensue about the penalty for a refusal, as if like real horses, eight- or nine-year-old boys were likely to approach a jump and refuse to attempt it. Whatever else, we were sticklers for the rules.

Ian O'Leary owned a digital watch so he was the official timekeeper except when it was his turn. Sometimes we just ran and jumped. Other days, we went full method acting. To get into character, we'd enthusiastically whack ourselves on the side of our arses with our right hands as we kept hold of the imaginary reigns with our left. I wonder now if any concerned parents were watching from their back windows, disturbed by this lunatic spectacle and worrying about our mental health as we snorted and galloped about or, rather embarrassingly, were tripped up by treacherous paint tins. I'm not sure if we ever went the whole way and started actually making neighing noises. If we did I think I may have long since made the subconscious decision to repress that memory.

I do know there were jump-offs where we raised the heights of the fences, well, paint tins and hurleys, and the boy who still went clear in the fastest time was declared the winner. If the result was in any way disputed, the loser might angrily give him the two fingers or, as we had learned to call it, give him the old Harvey Smith! Showjumping taught us that much at least.

Given our appetite for every possible sport, it was curious how some never tickled our fancy. Ireland won the Triple Crown when I was eleven years old. I watched the games live on RTÉ, cheered when I thought I was supposed to cheer but, in reality, I felt very little.

'Will they come to our school next week with the trophy and give us a half-day?' I asked my father.

'No boy, the likes of them won't be coming to *your* school,' he replied, the emphasis on 'your' the class warrior's way of teaching a child the difference between them and us.

Bizarrely and inexplicably it moved me as a spectacle less than the exploits of our national showjumping team. Then again, rugby seemed like a foreign game, something far removed from our world. Nobody we knew played it. Nobody we knew had ever played it. Therefore, for us, it didn't really exist.

Of course, Musgrave Park, Cork's premier rugby ground, was only a couple of miles up the road from our house in Ballyphehane. It was a venue of much curiosity for us. On the rare days when we ventured to watch Cork United at Turner's Cross and later Cork City games at Flower Lodge, myself, Barry Geoghegan and Stephen Mehigan often ventured in there if a match was going on. We did so with the demeanour of Japanese tourists pointing and smiling at the weird and wonderful sights available in this exotic corner of the sporting world.

We were impressed with the old stand because it looked like it was built by Subbuteo. And we were constantly amused by the strangeness of the rules (everybody clapped when somebody kicked the ball into touch) and then there was the players. They came in an assortment of shapes and sizes. Roly-poly guys who struggled to get around the field, fat jiggling beneath their shirts. Bean-poles with headbands and weird ear-wrappings who seemed impossibly tall. And there were always a few with thighs bulging out of their shorts as they gambolled up and down the field.

On winter afternoons, steam rose off the packs as they scrummed down, inching back and forth in the mud. We found this hilarious altogether, almost as funny as the sheepskin coats in the crowd intermittently baying 'heave'. After we had our fill of this strange spectacle, we headed out the gate and made for home along Connolly Road, amusing ourselves by shouting 'Heave' as the soundtrack to the rest of our journey.

If the reasons for my lack of interest in rugby were largely socio-cultural, there was no logical explanation for how basketball passed me by. I was thirteen when I got my first pair of Kareem Abdul-Jabbar basketball boots. They were fluorescent white with the three stripes of royal blue on each side. Like every other strange fashion decision I made in the 1980s (Parkas, Swiss Army jackets, Y cardigans, baggy Bowie pants), I beseeched my mother to buy them because everybody else had them. They looked good too, especially when worn beneath battleship-grey school uniform trousers on the way to and from Coláiste an Spioraid Naoimh each day.

I had no idea who Abdul-Jabbar was or what he stood for. I just liked the shoes. It was only when I saw the highlights of the NBA finals on RTÉ's *Sports Stadium* one time that I finally realised he was an American icon. Later, I learned enough of his amazing story of activism and protest off the court to be ashamed at how ignorant I was of his greatness. In my defence, it was basketball and I knew nothing at all about it even if one half of Cork was in utter thrall to the sport at that time.

I knew that it existed. I read the wall to wall coverage in the *Examiner* on Saturday mornings and the *Echo* on Saturday nights. It sounded like great fun altogether, especially the local derbies. Well, it sounded like great fun, except it was basketball, which to me was about as relevant as that other curio, rugby. How close did I come to it? I once saw a very tall, very handsome black man walking along Blarney Street when I was up there visiting my father's family home. I didn't recognise his face, but I presumed he was an American big man with one or other of the teams. What else would he have been doing there?

'I don't think the six by three tables are that good,' I said.

'The roll is very slow on them,' agreed Steve.

'The pockets are strangely set up too,' chipped in Barry.

We were discussing the various snooker tables that we knew and were very obviously lying to ourselves and to each other about their merits. The six-by-three-foot tables were far superior, and each of us would have killed to own one. But we didn't. We all had received Steve Davis fifty-four-inch by twenty-seven-inch models for Christmas that year, and so were busy persuading ourselves they were, in fact, superior to the larger alternative. What choice did we have?

We were standing in the bedroom that Barry shared with his two brothers, trying to figure out the best way to configure the table so we had the most room to play. There was no best way. The damned architects hired by Cork Corporation had not designed these houses with large-scale recreational items like this in mind. There was just one particular angle at which we were able to pull the cue back from a lot of places without banging against a wall or wardrobe or having to open the door. And that was good enough for us. We made do.

In tricky situations, snooker pros had to reach for the spider to balance the cue; we had to contend with holding the cue vertically instead of horizontally if the position was too near the wall. Same game, very different challenges. Pros probably didn't have to disassemble the table at the end of each session and slide it under their bed for fear of incurring the wrath of an angry mother either.

We were besotted by snooker for most of the 1980s. Here was a game we could play and could watch on television. When multi-channel came to our house in 1984, *Pot Black*, a weekly tournament involving the best players in the world, became one of our favourite shows. For a time too, there was a short lived comedy drama called *Give us a Break* where Paul McGann played a hot-shot with a cue trying to make a living off his talent in wide-boy London in the company of Robert Lindsay.

Myself and my friends loved it. It was like *Minder*, except with an improbable snooker-related storyline coursing through each episode. The problem was nobody else apparently thought much of it. It was yanked after one way-too-short season. To some, McGann will always be the I from 'Withnail and I'. To me, he was first and forever the Scouse ingénue Mo Morris.

We loved real snooker players too. Well, we loved some more than others. We could take or leave Ray Reardon, Terry Griffiths and Cliff Thorburn – too old, too serious, too slow. I wanted to be like Alex Higgins. After all, he was Irish and he was exciting, but it was difficult because my father kept up a stream of negative comments about him every time he played. This usually consisted of some combination of words like 'scut', 'corner-boy' and 'bowsie'.

I settled for supporting the younger players who most resembled Higgins, those with a bit of brash and brio like the perennial nearly-man Jimmy White and the troubled Kirk

Stevens. We watched the hirsute Canadian make the first ever live televised 147 during the Benson and Hedges in 1984. Not long after that, he went public with his cocaine addiction, and that was how my fourteen-year-old self learned about the existence of that particular drug. My mother may have subscribed to the old cliché that being good at snooker was a sign of a misspent youth but it was an education in its own way.

We were all united in our hatred of Steve Davis who, we agreed, simply bored his way to all those world championships. This showed how little we actually knew about the sport and the size of his talent. It also demonstrated what utter hypocrites we were. After all, we were happy enough to play on the table that he endorsed, the one with his smile and ginger hair on the box. Never mind that we looked faintly ridiculous theatrically chalking up the slender toy cues before every shot. Forget the difficulty involved in trying to inflict backspin on a white ball too small for that purpose.

The high point of the love affair with the game perhaps came when Dennis Taylor, the bespectacled man from Coalisland, defeated Davis in the 1985 final. That he triumphed on the final black of the final game made it all the sweeter. Finally, our nemesis had got his comeuppance. I went to bed that night deliriously happy and woke up the next day wondering if I'd have time to set up the table before heading off to school. The Steve Davis table, of course.

SIX

Do Not Adjust Your Set

We were sitting in the car. My mother and I. Smoke had started to fume from her ears with the frustration of waiting.

'Go in and get your father,' she said. The tone and the use of the word father denoted that my mother was annoyed. Seriously annoyed. I was only eight but I could tell that much already.

'Go in there and get him?' I asked from the back seat of the Vauxhall Viva. Surely she wasn't serious.

'Yes!' The voice was raised now. She was serious.

I opened the door and began to walk the ten yards from the kerb to the front door of John O'Mahoney's bookmakers. I'd sat vigil outside the betting office so many times as my dad went into there to gamble on the horses but I'd never ever been inside. Now, I was being told to go in search of a missing parent who had disappeared behind the mysteriously frosted-over windows and doors. I walked slowly, hoping my mother wasn't watching or wouldn't notice my deliberate attempt to fail at my task. I didn't want to cross this Rubicon. I wanted my father to emerge from the other side of the door just in time to spare me a glimpse behind the curtain.

At lunchtime on Saturdays, we drove to the top of Edward Walsh Road so my father could have a flutter and my mother could shop at Kelleher's, the conveniently located shop next door. There, she'd invariably run into some old neighbour from Ballyphehane while browsing the bargain aisle where recently out of date food and broken biscuits could be had at knock-down prices. This meant her trip around the store usually took longer than it should, making this the perfect arrangement. She shopped. He wagered. Problems arose when he gambled too long and she was left waiting outside. This was one of those days. And, for some reason, she was in no mood for waiting any longer.

The door was much heavier than it looked. Then again, it wasn't built for my puny eight-year-old arms. When I pushed my way in, nobody seemed to notice my arrival. All eyes were trained on a tiny screen mounted high in a corner where two walls met. Every man in the room was straining his eyes, watching tiny horses on some faraway distant racecourse jostling for position around a bend. Everybody in the rapt audience seemed to be clutching scraps of yellow paper in their fists. Some were rolling tiny pencils between their fingers, others had the little lead instruments perched on their ears, like carpenters preparing to measure a cut.

A tinny, disembodied English accent was coming through the speakers talking furlongs and favourites at a speed and in a language I knew my father spoke but I did not yet understand. A man was standing on a heightened platform carefully scratching numbers and lines onto a board. Every other remaining inch of wall space was papered over with the carefully-appointed racing pages from tabloids and broadsheets. Those I recognised.

I knew those black and white columns of meaningless numbers because I'd seen my dad pore over the agate type at the kitchen table, a suburban Bletchley Park code-breaker trying to read the runes and change his family's fortunes.

A cloud of smoke hung low from the ceiling. Older men with Brylcreemed hair sucked on the smouldering butts of cigarettes, clasping them tight between the thumbs and the forefingers of hands long ago stained mahogany by nicotine. Now and again, they blew philosophical wisps of blue in front of their faces, shaking their heads, crumpling a beaten docket in anger before hurling it to the floor. Boys not much older than myself, hard chaws I know my mother would have called them, huddled together in corners carefully etching 1s and 2s and Xs into the boxes alongside the names of English and Scottish teams on the football coupons.

I stood just inside the door taking it all in, afraid to venture any further into the lair. I didn't know it then but I had penetrated one of the great masculine sanctuaries, a demi-monde that made me both unnerved and excited in ways I was too young to understand. It reeked of tobacco, sweat, desperation and manhood. The only women in the room were employees, sitting behind the grille at the counter, taking bets and counting cash, collecting notes with one hand, handing back coins with the other.

There was a whiff of the illicit and the clandestine about the whole atmosphere. In a few years, I too would become a regular, like every other man and boy in the greater Togher metropolitan area between the ages of twelve and ninety. For now, though, my eyes were darting left and right, like a hunter searching my quarry, seeking out my father.

I found him perched on a stool by the back wall, deep in conversation with a man I didn't know. They appeared to be in a huddle, whispering, wearing the expressions of characters with some great conspiracy afoot. My father was reading aloud information from his copy of the *Daily Mirror* that was carefully folded open on the racing card pages. The other man was nodding his head sagely, writing something down on a fresh piece of two-fold white and yellow paper. I sidled across, slowly, anxious not to interrupt the exchange of obviously vital information.

'Dad! Dad!' I said, tugging his sleeve.

'Hello, boy, what's wrong with you?' he asked with the casual air of somebody who met his youngest son here all the time.

'Mam says we need to go,' I whispered. I'm not sure why I whispered. I guess some instinct told me this might spare him embarrassment.

'Is she finished inside?'

'She's finished a while, we're ready to go.'

I could see him surveying his options. 'Okay, boy,' he said, leaning into his co-conspirator, exchanging one more byte of crucial information before carefully folding a sheaf of dockets into the top pocket of his shirt and nodding at me that he was ready to go. In the car, my mother's complaints about his time-keeping were quickly fobbed off with promises of life-changing gambles that were about to pay off big and he drove home at great speed.

'Will you slow down?' she shouted as we turned left a little too sharply onto Togher Road.

'I can't,' he replied, 'we have to be home for the start of *Sports Stadium*.'

Sports Stadium ran on RTÉ television from 1972 until 1997. For half of that period we lived in one-channel land so it was, literally, the only show in town on Saturday afternoons. In a time before cable television it was the nearest we came to a sports channel, except it broadcast for just four to five hours per week. And, unfortunately, for much of the first decade of its existence, it seemed like most weeks ninety per cent of it was devoted to horse racing. Damned infernal horse racing.

The suits in RTÉ knew their audience. They knew my father.

From the moment Liam Nolan or Brendan O'Reilly came onscreen to introduce that day's fare – the gee-gees with a sprinkling of other stuff in between – he folded himself into the comfy armchair nearest to the fire, engrossed in live races from courses all over Britain and Ireland. Kempton. Uttoxeter. Epsom. Cheltenham. Leopardstown. Fairyhouse. I came to hate these bizarrely-named places. I came to hate horse racing. It monopolised the television, took up the large portion of what was supposed to be a sports show, and, almost on cue, broke my father's heart every seven days.

In this regard, his proximity to the flames was convenient because that's where most of his betting slips ended up. At the conclusion of a race, he might wait until the steward's enquiry then he'd give it one more careful read, a scholar running his eye over the exam for the last time, before flinging it into the fire in disgust. If Mam happened to be in the room, she reacted in different ways according to her mood. Sometimes, she smiled wryly and listened to his recurring tales of woe about a nag falling at the last, fading in the home stretch or being unfairly boxed in on the rail. Other days, she derided the whole business as 'a mug's game', saying something about 'fools being easily parted from their money.'

If he happened to have a winner, he'd rise and place the docket neatly in the frame of the mirror that hung over the mantelpiece. Above all the other trophies.

His own mood mostly ebbed rather than flowed with his fortunes. All manner of dark imprecations and curses were muttered under his breath and sometimes over it too. Individual jockeys came in for character assassination, trainers casually impugned for fixing races, and various ignoramuses and amadáns he met in the betting office vilified for passing on false leads. There was plenty of blame to go around. I wandered in and out of his orbit, not because of the always entertaining soap opera of his wagering but in search of the one thing that made *Sports Stadium* appointment television.

At a certain point each week, the incessant diet of horse racing was leavened by a brief interlude – a segment called Soccer Stadium. Wherever I was in the house or on the street, my father came calling, roaring at the top of his voice. He knew how much I looked forward to those twenty minutes. I sprinted to the couch in time to devour every second of one of the few outlets where televised soccer was available to us. If my mother wasn't gone to one of her many sisters' houses, she'd throw me in a slightly distressed Wagon Wheel, a fractured McVitie's United bar, or a bruised Penguin from her Kelleher's stash of misfit treats to heighten the enjoyment.

The best episodes of Soccer Stadium were those devoted to offering up the highlights package from the European soccer matches that had taken place in midweek. That we already knew the scores having listened to the action play out live on radio three days earlier did nothing to lessen the experience of being transported to foreign lands where everything about the game looked different from the sport we knew and loved.

These games invariably took place in cavernous stadia with running tracks necklacing the pitches, often with legions of armed guards and Alsatian dogs hovering menacingly in view. The height of exotica. Sometimes, in winter, daunting banks of snow the likes of which we'd never seen were piled up in front of the advertising hoarding behind the goals. Another wondrous sight.

Occasionally, the pitches were coated with frost and the ball used was orange. What a novelty. The shirts were a little odd too compared to what we were used to, and most of the goalkeepers wore tracksuit bottoms as they flapped at long-distance shots flying by. In Europe, the goals always seemed more spectacular or maybe that's the way I remember it.

Liverpool nearly always figured, usually on their trips behind the dreaded Iron Curtain. Again and again, my father tried to explain to me that there was no actual curtain though and this was merely a phrase popularised by Winston Churchill. Hardly an explanation to appeal to me. It was years before I understood that strange metaphor. I just preferred to see the Iron Curtain as a place where Liverpool went to eke out a score draw or scoreless draw to stamp their ticket to the next round.

In this regard, their consistent success helped an entire generation eventually come to understand the meaning of the away goals rule and the definition of the word 'aggregate'.

As Liverpool and, later and much more fleetingly, Nottingham Forest and Aston Villa swept all before them, we discovered the difference between Dynamo and Dinamo in faraway, alien cities like Kiev, Tbilisi and Minsk, and soaked up a knowledge of central and eastern European geography that stood to us through the rest of our education. In any primary school classroom, the soccer fans were the cosmopolitan sophisticates who could tell Bucharest from Budapest, not to mention being able to explain that Ajax was a famous Amsterdam nursery as well as a trusted brand of domestic cleaner that mothers kept under the sink.

Our imaginations fired up by what we had just seen on Soccer Stadium, we ran from our houses to meet in the square, recounting what we had just seen, mangling the pronunciation of the names of goalscorers and their clubs, and then doing our best to try to re-enact the highlights. Of course, it was always difficult to try to replicate an overhead kick or an acrobatic volley when you were playing on a hard, unforgiving concrete surface that tore skin on contact. Still, we gave it our best shot and for an hour every Saturday afternoon, we recast ourselves as peculiarly Cork-accented Olegs and Dimitris and Vasselys.

We also worshipped heroes closer to home. For a time *Sports Stadium* tried to live up to its actual billing by offering us other curios that didn't involve jockeys and whips and betting. The most memorable of these was Top Ace, a competition featuring the best handball players in Ireland, and, at one point, from America too. That we were mesmerised by this spectacle may have been because it was novel and entertaining or it could just have been that it wasn't horse racing. At a certain juncture in my childhood, croquet might have provided a welcome relief from the blasted sport of kings.

What was amazing about our relationship with handball is that it was purely televisual. We had never seen it live. Indeed, the first time I even saw a handball alley was much later, when I started to play Gaelic football with Coláiste an Spioraid Naoimh, and spent interminable Wednesday afternoons making long trips to depressing, vaguely sinister boarding schools in rural backwaters. Complete ignorance of the game and its culture didn't prevent us from sitting down to watch Top Ace. Much to the chagrin of my father.

'Why don't we play handball?' I asked.

'That's only a game for country boys,' he replied on the way out to the kitchen. He was a man inordinately proud of his urban heritage, like only somebody whose entire family had lived within the Cork city limits for several generations could be. 'Call me when it's over and the racing is back on.'

Despite his disapproval, we came to know the finest exponents of the art, men like Dick Lyng and Pat Kirby, who wore short shorts and singlets (sometimes in their county colours), flinging themselves around a court with a glass wall at the back for the cameras. We learned the rules and the difference between 60 by 30 and 40 by 20 from Mick Dunne and we thought the whole thing strangely fascinating. The occasional presence of an American (or 'feckin' Yank!' as my father described them when he deigned to watch with me) lent an ersatz glamour that drew us in further.

Nobody in our extended family on either my mother's or father's side had ever been to America. This made Terry Muck and the sprinkling of other Midwestern competitors objects of curious fascination to us. Some of them wore headbands, sweatbands and goggles, strange accoutrements that made them look even more alien than they sounded in post-match interviews.

The paucity of live soccer was such that in 1980 I'd get excited and/or called into the room when a Coca-Cola commercial came on television. Why? Because it featured tanned Americans playing soccer in a park bathed in the kind of sunshine we only saw for a few fleeting hours every summer. The star of the show was a boy around my age whom I hated and admired in equal measure, depending on my mood. This precocious character looked like he'd walked straight off the set of an episode of *CHiPs* and a later urban myth reckoned it was the first role played by Ralph Macchio, the original Karate Kid.

Certainly the lad had the deft footwork of somebody fluent in a martial art because he performed all manner of impressive tricks with the ball. He was flicking it with his left repeatedly, managing to pull off a game of headers with an equally talented friend, and then volleying it back and forth with somebody who might have been his dad. I wanted to emulate him. I wanted to kill him.

All of this played out in a perfectly manicured park where he was surrounded by what seemed like his entire extended family on some sort of picnic – even his grandmother was smiling at his antics. The latter detail troubled me greatly because I knew for a fact if I was juggling a ball in the vicinity of my nan I'd be shooed off by her or my mother or the small army of vigilant aunts who served as her very own praetorian guard.

For a while, I was a tad obsessed with the Coca-Cola kid, jealous of his ability, his amazing technicolour lifestyle and his profile. I remember going on and on to my poor mother about how it would be easier for him to get scouted by an English club since he was always on the telly. I also beseeched her to buy me a yellow t-shirt just like his because it made him look Brazilian.

When she refused, all I could do was go out into the front garden to practice the especially audacious piece of skill that ended the commercial, which involved him flinging himself airborne and executing a perfect overhead kick. That the ball ended up going to the legion of admirers who were following him around this bucolic park rather than into a goal mattered not a jot. I was too besotted by the acrobatics involved so I spent hours trying to replicate this feat.

Nothing tires a nine-year-old out like repeatedly hurling yourself skyward attempting an overhead kick on a mucky front lawn the size of a postage stamp. Not to mention either that, unlike the American boy wonder, my efforts were not rewarded with a Coke and a smile, but with a dressing-down from an angry mother irate at the mud on the back of my shirt.

I felt similar envy towards a group of kids who cropped up as regulars on *Youngline*, the one half an hour per week that RTÉ devoted to young people's programming. A few minutes of each show every Thursday was devoted to a video of a Dutch coach called Wiel Coerver doing soccer training drills with boys not much older than myself on perfectly manicured fields. Again, I watched for several different reasons: to soak up this smidgen of soccer onscreen, to copy the drills in order to improve my skills and to grow impossibly jealous of these brats.

Inevitably, I was convinced all that stood between me and making it as a professional one day was a few sessions with this sage from the low countries, delivering heavily-accented instructions in a way that made him sound serious and rigorous. Just what I needed to improve. Decades later, I learned Coerver was one of the most progressive youth coaches in the world; father of a method of teaching that still bears his name, and in providing us with access to his teaching RTÉ was truly fulfilling its public service remit.

Back then, my main concern was figuring out how to be one of the boys who got to work with him on the show. I once sat down and wrote a letter to *Youngline* outlining why I'd be perfect for the slot. They never wrote back. Not even Pat Butler, the presenter with the Cork accent, bothered to put pen to paper. I later found out they couldn't possibly have replied because my mother admitted she never actually mailed my missive.

I forgave her because it wasn't like she didn't indulge my passion for the beautiful game. On Wednesday nights, she'd holler for me if a soccer player like Pat Jennings or Peter Shilton was being stalked by Eamon Andrews and his red book at the start of *This is Your Life*, one of her most beloved shows each week. She adored the almost obligatory rags to riches biography of the subject. My father hated it, dismissing it as a mutual admiration society before reminding me every single week that the great Danny Blanchflower once told Andrews to shove his red book. This story might have impressed me more if I had ever seen Blanchflower play.

My father spent most episodes of the show exiled in the back kitchen. He'd put Marty Robbins on the record player just loud enough so that we could hear it in the television room and sit there tearing into some Eric Van Lustbader novel about ninjas, one of his peculiar obsessions. Meanwhile, every schmaltzy anecdote or teary memory recalled by one of Andrews's guests was invariably and awkwardly soundtracked by 'Big Iron on his Hip' or 'The Cowboy in the Continental Suit' wafting through the walls.

Everybody in the house was attuned to my appetite for soccer, any soccer. One Thursday evening my sisters called me in to where they were worshipping at the altar of *Top of the Pops*. They thought I might like it because some Scottish guy called BA Robertson was kicking a ball up and down the stage while singing a song that actually had soccer-themed lyrics. I traipsed around the house for days afterwards singing the most memorable lyrics ever learned by an eight-year-old.

> *'Knocked it off, you know I knocked it off,*
> *While I was sitting in the corner with my tracksuit off*
> *I was hopin' I'd be playin'*
> *But I never thought I'd be winnin' the game.'*

That a few scraps of sepia-tinted footage on *This Is Your Life* or ball-kicking antics on *Top of the Pops* were regarded as something to feast on sums up the poverty of our viewing options when we had only one and then two RTÉ channels. A few times a year, there were Ireland internationals shown live on a Wednesday afternoon, fixtures that required a sprint from the classroom once the dismissal bell rang and a maternal understanding that homework would have to wait. Every May, there was a glut of (well, three) live matches as we gorged ourselves on the finals of the European Cup Winners' Cup, the European Cup and the FA Cup. We prayed for replays in the latter game to give us one more ninety minutes to savour.

All of the above will explain why, years before the Catholic Church introduced Saturday night mass, that particular evening already contained the most religious experience of my week. *Match of the Day* came on around 11.20pm, ridiculously late for a young child but, especially before we bought our first VHS video recorder, it was appointment television. It could not be missed. Under any circumstances. And this meant there were delicate negotiations with my parents and special arrangements made so I would be in situ to hear the theme music that was the soundtrack to so many of our sporting dreams.

'Da da da daa dadata data…' went the number composed by Barry Stoller in 1970, a year before I was born. I never knew his name but Stoller was our Beethoven. Our Mozart. Our Liszt. He moved us every time we heard those notes. This song was simply the sound of joy and breathless anticipation, signalling the start of maybe fifty glorious minutes of soccer highlights. When I lashed a ball against the wall in the driveway, 'Da da da daaa dadata data…' was playing in my head and sometimes I sang it out loud if nobody else was around. I had nothing to be ashamed of. Every other kid was just as affected by that tune.

The build-up to *Match of the Day* began many hours before that emotional music played and Jimmy Hill's distinctive chin and beard hovered into view. There were many obstacles to be overcome before we reached that point because Saturday night was bath night in our house. Afterwards, we sat, reluctantly, on a kitchen chair placed in front of the fire as my mother blow-dried our hair ('or else you'll catch your death of cold!' she warned).

Then the clock started ticking. At 9pm, the RTÉ news came on, the headlines almost invariably about bloody events in Ulster, and that meant it was time for me to head upstairs to bed. Every anxious step of the way, I was assured that I would be woken the moment *The Late Late Show* ended.

'Once Gay says goodnight, we'll come up and get you,' assured my mother. I knew from a young age Gay Byrne was as important to her as Jimmy Hill was to me. His involvement, however tangential, in the covenant between us assuaged my fears.

If she was always the guarantor, it was my father who inevitably did the heavy lifting. Because that's what was involved. He'd wake us with a whisper and a hand on the shoulder. Then he'd carry Tom and me down from our sleeping beds and place us bleary-eyed, stretching in front of the dying embers of the coal fire. Tom took the couch. My spot was on the rug on the floor leaning against my father's legs. He produced a few dry sticks or a couple of lumps of coal and these were judiciously placed to rekindle the blaze, just enough to ignite flames to keep us warm past midnight.

Some evenings, my father might be freshly returned from a game of Don in Flannery's Bar at the top of Clashduv Estate, the distinctive hoppy aroma of Murphy's Stout on his breath and a little mischief in his eyes. Those nights, he ignored the many stern warnings issued by my mother earlier in the evening and headed into the kitchen at a certain point in the show to see what was cooking. Returning triumphantly, he balanced unwieldy sandwiches made from carving delicious slivers from the Sunday roast basting in the oven. No meat ever tasted as good as those contraband cuts consumed on those late night vigils together. No televised football ever seemed as magical.

We saw goals that were imprinted on our memories forever. I over-celebrated any scored against Liverpool because it tormented my brother but even he was left open-mouthed by Justin Fashanu's effort for Norwich City. The most spectacular production I ever saw on *Match of the Day*.

The ball was fed to the burly number 9 at pace on an uneven pitch; he controlled it nonchalantly with his right as he turned on the edge of the box, then let fly with his left on the volley. I was behind the couch within seconds trying to volley a cushion in a similar fashion against the wall. Every child on the street spent weeks afterwards trying and failing to recreate the whole movement, right down to the arc of the ball on its way past the outstretched hand of Ray Clemence.

Then there was the night Keith Weller wore white tights for Leicester City against Norwich City. It was an FA Cup match in winter and we were informed by the bemused commentary team that he had chosen to do so to insulate his legs against the cold. This sounded logical enough – even to an eight-year-old – and he scored in that match too, so it obviously didn't impede him any. The strangest part of the night was *Match of the Day* ending with a brief sequence of Weller's footwork set to ballet music. My father thought that especially hilarious.

Jimmy Hill was as much an icon to us as any of the players. I remember seeing the actor Brian Murphy on an episode of the sitcom *George and Mildred* drawing a Hill goatee and moustache on a mirror so he could see what he looked like with that kind of facial hair. I searched high and low, through drawers and all around my sisters' bedroom, until I found a marker so I could do the same in our bathroom. Hill may have sounded like a strict headmaster but he opened the door to our dreams every Saturday night.

Once a month, we salivated as he introduced the Goal of the Month contenders. 'Goal A scored by Ian Rush for Liverpool versus...' Every single time Tom and I argued our choices and then resolved to put our selections on a post card and mail it off to the BBC in Shepherd's Bush, wherever that was. Every month that earnest midnight resolution didn't survive into Sunday morning. And when the results were announced we were always filled with regret about our failure to enter this competition.

In spring, the Easter Saturday night edition of the programme was rendered especially spiritual because it also marked the end of our Lenten fast. In our family, we always gave up sweets for the forety days and, according to ecclesiastical law (or my mother's perhaps rather loose post-Vatican II interpretation of it at least), the penance ended at midnight on Holy Saturday.

As the old wooden clock on the mantelpiece ticked towards midnight, my father assured us it was running a few minutes slow, thereby allowing us to pare further time off our penance. After forty days, every second counted. This meant the three of us watched the last part of that particular *Match of the Day* while stuffing our faces with squares from the giant Cadbury's bars – the eggs having been deemed too sacrosanct for a premature feast. Just the type of nutrition a young boy needs when heading back to bed in the wee small hours of the morning.

Sometimes on Saturday nights we were shooed up to bed the moment the credits rolled. But on cold nights, in the years before central heating arrived to warm our hearts, he'd send us to get our, by then, tepid hot water bottles so he could refill them with freshly boiled water. As we waited for the kettle to sing in the kitchen, we'd dawdle by the telly so that we could see the playing of the national anthem, a bizarre coda to the night's entertainment.

There was no 'Sinne Fianna Fáil, atá fé gheall ag Éirinn…', just an orchestra playing Peader Kearney's tune over a reel of classic images: waves cascading towards the shore, streams trickling over rocks, cobwebs glistening on tree branches and a butterfly fluttering its wings on a leaf. All manner of flora and fauna culminating in a glorious sunset over a mountain that seemed to rise out of the sea.

'Why do they show that?' I asked.

'To remind us how beautiful Ireland is,' replied my father.

SEVEN

We Can Be Heroes

By 1979 my father had got a job at Pfizer's Pharmaceuticals in Ringaskiddy. For a man with no trade or training, it paid well, mostly because it involved shift work and the handling of dangerous chemicals. The latter part of the gig meant he only lasted a couple of years, and we all later blamed that stint for the health problems that afflicted him for the rest of his life. This temporary boon to the family finances also impacted on our various routines. Since he had to drive to the factory down in Cork harbour, we now had to walk more. Which was fine until we were forced to walk places we didn't want to go – like mass on a Sunday morning.

In the summer of that year, I remember my mother hunting myself and Tom up the road to 9:30am mass at the SMA church in Wilton, SMA somehow standing for the Society of African Missions. Being just eight and eleven, we were not yet bold or brave enough to skip it altogether. We feared being unable to answer a question about which priest said mass or what the homily was about.

Still, we were reluctant enough congregants that we always took the long way around, dawdling as much as we could on the tree-lined roadway that wended its way through the back of the church grounds. Aside from hopefully making us late enough to shave a few minutes off this torturous ordeal, there was an off-chance we might see somebody from Ghana or Nigeria walking in the grounds between the chapel and the accommodation behind it.

This was, of course, a huge novelty at this time. Since we knew no better, we'd stop and stare wide-eyed at the exotic sight of a young African novice walking across our path, carrying on regardless, hopefully oblivious to our ignorant gawping.

Throughout that particular year, the trip to mass became marginally more exciting because work was being fast completed on the construction of a vast temple of commerce on land directly in front of the church. Each week we gauged the progress of this building, and by autumn there were four huge W-shaped entrances. I told Tom they reminded me of Wembley. He told me to shut up and stop being ridiculous.

Of course, it actually stood for Wilton Shopping Centre, and outlandish rumours abounded about the various glittering emporiums the place would contain when it was finally done. The only one that concerned us was the talk of a sports shop. Just a mile walk from our house. A sports shop! Imagine – with nothing but sports stuff!

By the time December came and the official grand opening of Wilton was finally announced, we knew that the rumours were true. Perhaps the only time in our entire childhood a rumour proved true. We knew the truth of it before we ever set foot in the place because, amid much hype and hoopla, we learned the shop of our dreams was to be known as 'Johnny Giles' Sports'. Not only that, Johnny Giles himself, the actual soccer player, the player, the manager, the legend, would even be present for the opening and available to sign autographs.

This was, by some distance, the most exciting event to happen anywhere near our house for the entire decade. There was talk of nothing else on the street or in the schoolyard except the imminent arrival of Johnny Giles. Perhaps it was a measure of his standing in the game that we never seemed to refer to him by anything other than his full name. As if this wasn't exciting enough, somebody with a more creative imagination than most of us put it out there that he'd be arriving by helicopter and landing in the vast car park. This was too much for us to fathom. The glamour of it.

Of course, he didn't descend from the heavens, or at least I don't think he did. I have no idea how he got there. All I know is that when Tom and I arrived at Wilton that evening and saw a queue stretching out one of the main doors, underneath one of those giant Ws, we didn't have to ask what it was for. It was a queue made of young boys, clutching scraps of paper and notebooks, and a sprinkling of increasingly impatient-looking fathers.

I took my place in the line and scoffed disdainfully at the stuff some boys had brought the great man to sign. See, I had, in my hands, an actual autograph book, a slim, weirdly shaped affair that came free with the first edition of *Scoop!* magazine, a short-lived rival to *SHOOT!*. I prized this tome because it was such a professional production that it even said 'Autograph Book' on the cover – just in case anyone was wondering.

After what seemed like three days waiting, I finally got in the door of the shop and saw Johnny Giles sitting behind a table. I only glanced at him briefly because my eye was taken by the smorgasbord of sporting goods on every wall. I was in heaven. There were tracksuits, soccer balls, basketballs, Gaelic footballs and an entire rack of Sondico goalkeeper gloves, just like the ones sold in the ads in *SHOOT!*. So much to take in. So little time.

'It's your turn,' said the woman in charge, ushering me towards my audience with the great man.

He smiled at me and signed my autograph book although surprisingly enough he failed to acknowledge how much more prepared I was than the other amateurs with their scraps of paper. Then he nodded, a signal that I took was the gesture for me to move on. There were still hundreds behind me waiting in the queue for their brush with sporting celebrity.

I walked out of Wilton, looking at his signature though, and felt kind of deflated without knowing exactly why.

'Was it exciting?' asked my mother when I got home.

'Yes, it was,' I lied, handing her the book for inspection.

She was unimpressed by the penmanship of his autograph.

'His writing is worse than Dr McKenna's. Still, at least you got to meet one of your heroes.'

She was wrong. And I knew then why I felt strangely unimpressed. Johnny Giles was not my hero. How could he have been? I never remembered seeing him on *Match of the Day* with Leeds United in his heyday. I was too young for that. And I had only the briefest, vaguest recall of him in an Ireland shirt, standing in midfield, pointing a lot. He was a perfectly polite individual during our brief transaction, but to me, he was just a well-dressed man with a very strong hand. After all, he must have signed his name a thousand times that night!

This is the thing with heroes though. They can't be foisted upon you. You must find your own and that's an organic process that takes time and often happens in strange ways. I was eight that night, far too young to appreciate the midfield genius that was Johnny Giles, and far too ignorant of Irish soccer history to understand his place in its pantheon. My father and my uncles and even my mother (who knew nothing of the sport) all assured me he was a great. I had even heard adults discussing his greatness in the queue at Wilton that night as well.

So I knew it to be true. And I knew he was worth revering but I had to find icons for myself. And I did.

For a time I had a minor, fleeting obsession with a boxer called Dave Boy Green. I think it was based on two things. His name was Dave. Just like me. And myself and my father listened to a couple of his fights on the radio on Wednesday nights on the BBC's Light Programme. Too young to have stayed up for the Ali-Frazier-Foreman epics, I was bizarrely smitten by this welterweight from Cambridge. They called him 'The Fen Tiger', and my father took a long time explaining what a fen was to me. He usually fought at the Royal Albert Hall, but I'd outgrown the relationship by the time Green was outclassed by Sugar Ray Leonard, somewhere in America in 1980. That bout took place in a time zone that ensured the first I knew of the defeat was when my father showed me a report in the *Daily Mirror*, and muttered the words 'out of his depth'.

Not long after that, Gary Shaw, the Aston Villa striker, became the object of my affections. This was a byproduct of my passion for his club and that was born out of sheer bitterness. On 17 December 1976 I was a month shy of my sixth birthday when I witnessed my father break the news to Tommy that Villa had trounced his beloved Liverpool 5–1, a result that also yielded what fans claim was the best half of football in the Birmingham club's history.

When I witnessed my brother's anger and dismay at Liverpool's loss, I tried to compound it by declaring myself a Villa fan. I just wanted to be able to rub it in that little bit more. Never mind how pathetic I must have sounded. Any way of scoring points against him was legitimate. So, too young and too naïve to grasp that this result was an anomaly, I became a Villa man, or boy at least. The most ridiculous and costly decision I could have made. For one hour of mockery, I opened myself up to a lifetime of hurt, and I was almost certainly the only non-Manchester United fan in Cork who hated Liverpool enough to boycott their friendly against a Republic of Ireland XI at Flower Lodge in 1986.

My suffering was punctuated by brief and fleeting occasions of glory, and most of those involved Gary Shaw in the early 1980s. I started to cut photographs of him from *SHOOT!* and from any of the tabloids my father brought home. I carefully blue-tacked them to the bedroom walls, avoiding my brother's side at all cost, lest the blond-mopped goal machine in claret and blue impinge upon the Liverpool section of the room. When Shaw started to write a weekly column for *SHOOT!* I felt our bond growing closer and imagined that his (presumably ghost-written) account of his rather humdrum life was personally addressed to me. I searched every missive in vain for clues about how to improve my own game. The only thing I learned was to try to avoid getting the type of catastrophic injuries that destroyed his career.

That exaggerated sense of my closeness to Shaw was born of my desperation to forge any tangible link with the English scene because that was the stuff of all our soccer dreams. To that end, my father's next stop on his career carousel, after his chest proved unable to tolerate being around vats of chemicals every day, was to prove an especially lucky break for me.

Briefly, he found work as a security guard for Securicor and was assigned to a newly-constructed yet empty ESB plant near our home. After school some afternoons I'd rush through my homework so I could walk over to accompany him back from the 8am to 4pm shift. Along the way, we shot the breeze about the sporting issues of the moment that obsessed us both. On occasion, I arrived early at the hut and hung out with him there in what was obviously a blatant breach of protocol.

Those days, he'd brew a pot of tea and I'd dunk a couple of Rich Tea biscuits in a mug while marvelling at the sophisticated walkie-talkie and super-powerful flashlight that were part of his basic equipment. Sometimes, the man to take over his watch was a quietly-spoken figure who arrived on a bicycle. My father introduced him to me first as somebody whose son was an apprentice footballer at Leeds United. The billing took my breath away.

The man's name was Justin Irwin, his child was Denis. As an eleven-year-old boy in 1982, for whom listening to James Alexander Gordon calling out the classified check on BBC radio every Saturday afternoon had become as sacred a ritual as the Angelus, this was the closest I had yet come to the impossible glamour of the English game.

It didn't matter that Denis Irwin was then shuttling around the netherworld of Elland Road reserve and youth teams, his was a name for me to conjure with. Liam Brady may have been a superstar in Italy then, converting the penalty to win the Scudetto for Juventus, and Ronnie Whelan had just broken into the all-conquering Liverpool team, but they were Dubliners. In the Cork suburb of Togher in the early '80s, that was a different world, the capital city being, in my imagination, as far away from us as any English town.

Around about this time, Kieran O'Regan, another Corkman, started to break through to the first team at Brighton and Hove Albion. I was interested in him too, but never smitten. After all, even though Irwin was a couple of rungs below O'Regan on the career ladder, I now knew his father. Well, kind of. Sort of.

More importantly, Irwin came from a house a couple of hundred yards away from my own. We shared a postal address. I knew this because, doing my best Jim Rockford impression, I found out exactly where he lived in Argideen Lawn on the Deanrock Estate. I made it my business to stroll past it all the time on my way to St Finbarr's GAA club – just in case I'd spot him.

Not that far-fetched a notion. During the close season, he often turned up at the club where he had once been a promising hurler to revisit old friends and team-mates. One glorious summer's evening, I spent a good five minutes staring at him from twenty yards away as he stood, oblivious to my gaze, watching a hurling match from the grassy bank that abutted the old number one pitch. I thought about going down the autograph road, but I was sixteen by then and had stopped carrying the *Scoop!* autograph book with me everywhere.

It's not that I had matured like a normal adolescent or anything. Every time I played on that elevated ground near Cork Airport against Everton, the schoolboy outfit where Irwin had made his name just a few years earlier, I fantasised about him showing up there, spotting some latent talent in me that nobody else ever could, and immediately alerting the scouts about this left-footed diamond in the rough.

In terms of hero worship, it scarcely mattered either that Leeds United eventually let him go (worst decision ever), and Oldham Athletic, his next destination, was never quite box office. He came from around our way, was still playing for pay, in England, and that was enough to fire my rabid teenage imaginings.

In the pre-Sky Sports era, a time before newspapers figured that sports supplements and blanket coverage of soccer made commercial sense, myself and my father scoured the English

Sundays for team listings and any detail that might enlighten us as to how Irwin had performed the previous day. Every now and again, the *Evening Echo* or *Cork Examiner* did a lengthy interview with him that I cut out and placed between the pages of a fading, half-full Panini sticker album from the 1980 European Championships. Like the teen music aficionado who first discovers a band when they are indie darlings playing basement bars then watches them go on to fill stadiums, I savoured that collection as evidence that my passion for Irwin predated his glory years at Manchester United.

It may well have been in one of those clippings I first read that Irwin's own sporting hero was Jimmy Barry-Murphy. He was Barrs. He was Cork. Who else could it be?

See, I had many heroes with a small h. Only one could have been spelt with a capital H. That exalted status was reserved for Jimmy. Jimmy Barry-Murphy. JBM. The man with three names wasn't just my hero. Or Irwin's. He belonged to every boy who came of age in Cork around that time and to some smarter kids with taste from far beyond our county bounds. We all attended rival schools, played for warring GAA clubs, and wore different colours at the weekends. We all worshipped at the altars of the various English soccer clubs. But we all had in common the one true God. And he was different than all other deities because he walked among us.

Colm Ó Loingsigh was the visionary principal of Scoil Mhuire Gan Smál in Glasheen. An impossibly tall, thin man, he seemed to use his long legs to stride at great pace up and down the corridors and the stairs of our primary school. He had the kind of lofty stature that makes kids think twice about stepping out of line. At one point, we began using a book called *Illustrated Civics 1* and somebody noticed his name on the cover. He had written it. Himself. For a boy like me, with a nascent interest in words and books, this was the most amazing thing. Somebody in our school had written a book. With his name on it and everything. A book that was bought by people to use in classrooms. Maybe even to read.

If that wasn't enough to impress me, Mr Lynch, as we called him, was also in charge of hurling in the school. In early September in fifth class, all interested boys were invited to start training for the team. Our first session took place immediately after school in the nearby rugby training grounds of Presentation Boys' Secondary School. A rolling herd of us half-walked, half-ran the short distance. We'd been going to school matches for years. Here now was our chance to take the first step down the road to wearing the light-blue jersey (which looked a little too like the Dublin shirt for my liking) that had been worn with distinction by our older brothers and the bigger boys on our street.

We gathered by the dressing-rooms that we weren't allowed to use and we waited. Then a familiar sight hove into view. The brand-new Fiat Mirafiori of Mr Lynch. We recognised it from afar because he was one of the only people in our world who had a new car. We swarmed around him as he got out and then he made us line up while he opened the boot. That was when we gasped. It was full to the brim with hurleys. Ash wands of all shapes and sizes. Some were beaten-up and might have been put to better use as kindling. Others were in perfect nick. A few were the dreaded Wavin white plastic jobs.

We stood by the back of the car until he found one that fit

each of us, the optimum measurement being the top of the handle reaching the hip bone when the *bas* was stood on the ground. Those of us who had hurled before knew what a proper hurley was supposed to look like, the grain curving around the bas. We showcased that knowledge as we examined them like wine snobs eyeing a label.

The arrivistes in our midst, those who knew no better, expressed a preference for the white of the Wavin because they were shinier and looked like the type of weapon a bad guy might be wielding on *Blake's Seven,* the spectacularly low-rent yet still magnificent English sci-fi television show that was a staple of our Sunday night viewing. They all found out the hard way how much the fibreglass stung your hands every time you hit the ball.

Those, like me, who had hurled before made a big deal of road-testing our choices with pretend shots, affected pre-pubescent golfers warming up on an imaginary tee box. The less-experienced started using theirs as lightsabres and as swords. Indeed, some of them would subsequently be placed on the edge of the square in matches where they'd slash and swipe at everything that moved, fulfilling all their Skywalker fantasies and occasionally, almost accidentally, inveigling a goal or two.

Eventually, when every boy was suitably armed, Mr Lynch began the process of trying to teach us the rudiments of hurling. A tough job, it required infinite patience, especially on a rugby field where the sliotar was often entrapped by thick grass that badly needed another trim. Particularly onerous conditions for trying to pass on the joys of the ground game. That first year we went nowhere but twelve months on, after so much well-meaning instruction and occasional wincing from our coach, a journey that began so inauspiciously that afternoon came to a wonderful end.

On a windy autumn day, on a field behind St Joseph's School on the Mardyke, we defeated St Vincent's and won a Sciath na Scol title before a baying crowd of our schoolmates and theirs. Late on in the match, I got a hurley in the face, the metal splice opening the skin above my top lip, an injury that required my premature departure and a trip to the Mercy Hospital for stitches. The type of excessively dramatic cameo that ensured my contribution to the victory was greatly exaggerated thereafter. A good age to learn shedding blood for the cause will almost always do that.

What mattered most about that triumph, though, happened months later in the dead of winter. Mr Lynch appeared in Mr Nelligan's class one morning to announce there would be a formal medal presentation ceremony in the school gym. It would be held at night, our parents were invited and the guest of honour, the man to give us our precious baubles, would be Jimmy Barry-Murphy. This was more thrilling than winning any game or championship. HE was coming to our school. To our gym. To see us. Imagine telling an eleven-year-old today Lionel Messi was on his way to speak to the class. That level of delirium.

I don't remember much about the evening. Just that Jimmy smiled a lot and shook a lot of hands. He must have spoken some words of wisdom. I didn't hear any of them. I was too busy battling my nerves ahead of finally meeting my hero. Eventually, Mr Lynch, the MC for the evening, started his way through the team, Mark McCarthy in goal, onwards… When he came to me, I took a deep breath, and shuffled towards the top of the room. He handed me the medal and smiled. Actually, I'm not sure if he smiled because I kept my head down the whole time.

His grip felt strong as he shook my hand and handed me my trophy. Then I made my way back to my seat. Relieved. Lighter. Walking on air. Wearing a stupid grin that stayed in place for hours afterwards. I had, finally, breathed the same air as my hero.

Jimmy Barry-Murphy finished his playing career with six All-Ireland medals, five hurling, one football, and seven All-Stars. He won every national available title at minor, Under-21 and senior in both codes. Yet the details of his successes scarcely matter as much as the manner of them. He just did things differently than everybody else.

I was too young to remember him in his first incarnation as a skin-headed, teenage, goal-scoring sensation with the fabled footballers of 1973. I have only a vague memory of him accompanying Liam McCarthy to our school in 1976 and 1977 when I was five and six. But I can never remember a time when he was not my hero.

Older men tried to burst my bubble, telling me that Jimmy was great and all but there were better hurlers. Christy Ring, of course, was the prime example. The empirical evidence indicates that this is true. Ring won more. Ring was greater. But Ring wasn't ours. Ring was my father's hero. That was the generation he belonged to. My father could tell a story about Ring and bookend it with seeing the great man driving his oil lorry on some country road the next day. Entertaining enough fare but to me, he was the stuff of sepia-tinted footage. Impressive. Yet distant. Faraway.

Jack Lynch was another name the elders liked to conjure with, brought up to remind us young fellas that Cork didn't begin and end with Jimmy. I heard all the yarns about the Glen Rovers man winning six consecutive All-Irelands between 1941 and 1946 (the football in 1945 punctuating the hurling triumphs) but it barely registered. To me, he was an old man in a suit that my mother pointed out to me in Daunt's Square one afternoon when he was on the campaign stump with Liam Ó Murchú during a general election.

She was extremely disappointed when I was unimpressed by the sight of this smiling, genial character shaking hands as dozens orbited around him and traffic came to a standstill as cars slowed to take a closer look at the kerfuffle. I knew he was important, but it was difficult to conceive of him as a swashbuckling athlete who famously caught the number 16 bus from Terenure to Croke Park on his way to starring for Cork in the 1945 final. Not when my only memory of him was a politician glad-handing voters and slapping backs, and preventing me from persuading my mother to buy me dinner at Mandy's Fast Food Emporium.

Jimmy was different than these old men. He was a living, breathing, technicolour idol. Lynch and Ring were the stuff of legend but it was somebody else's legend. We witnessed Jimmy do things that allowed all of us to compile our own personal highlight reel. This was not a story handed down to us by our forefathers. This was an icon of our very own that we watched evolve before our eyes. In him, the word was made flesh.

On the first Sunday in May 1980 Cork and Limerick battled it out for the National Hurling League title at Páirc Uí Chaoimh. This was a strange occasion. Still basking in the glow of the county's recent three-in-a-row All-Irelands, the team or the fans didn't usually take the winter competition too seriously. Established players, especially JBM, often went into hibernation, allowing unproven youngsters to try to prove their mettle on soft pitches before sparse crowds.

Whatever set of circumstances aligned that year, the final was fixed for Cork so my father decided we would go. There was a kind of unspoken agreement that he had to bring us to all matches that took place there because he never had a car sufficiently reliable enough to make it across the county boards to Thurles or Dublin for the real glamour fixtures. A source of constant tension between us.

The game ended in a draw and at some point during our epic post-match walk to Capwell to be picked up by my mother, he announced that if the replay was on at the same venue we'd be there again. If JBM was now taking the league seriously, he figured, then so should we. Seven days later, we took our seats in the open stand (he was working in Pfizer's at the time so he was flush enough to move from the Blackrock End). That was my vantage point for perhaps the most Jimmy moment in the history of Jimmy.

It was in the second half of an encounter about which I remember nothing else. At this point, Jimmy took possession and embarked on a solo run. Three opponents set off in hot pursuit as he hared towards goal. Then Jimmy suddenly stopped dead in his tracks and put his hands on his hips. My eyes, and everybody else's, looked back to where he had come from and there was Pat Horgan in the last act of dispatching the ball over the bar.

All around us, adults, like bemused forensic scientists happening upon a crime scene, tried to piece together the extraordinary series of events. Eventually, some consensus was reached and my father explained to us. It was the perfect dummy. On the way through, Jimmy had dropped the ball on his blindside where the defenders couldn't see it and kept running towards goal. Of course, they followed him and this allowed Horgan to pick it up unhindered for an easy score. A fleeting moment where vision, daring, class and touch were manifest in a sleight of hand nobody else would have even thought of, much less attempted. Classic JBM.

That's how I remember it anyway. I've never seen footage and I don't want to. It's too perfect in my nine-year-old mind. The cleverest trick I'd ever seen pulled on a field and all done so that somebody else could enjoy a moment of glory. This was not some Neymaresque fancy performed far from goal for the benefit of the crowd either. This was magic with a purpose. Discreet sorcery designed simply to bamboozle defenders and create an easy opening... for a team-mate.

The circumstances of that moment capture what made Jimmy special, different, unique. Who else would have thought of that? Who else would have tried it? What Barry-Murphy had was intangible. It was star power yet famously, everybody who ever met him vouchsafed that he had no ego. Matches were turned or lit up with these almost fantastical improvisations, so many improbable dramatic flourishes, yet he carried himself in such a modest way that it never looked to be about him.

I was mesmerised by his wristwork, fascinated by the slippery manner in which he turned this way and that when he first took possession to shake off defenders. He wasn't particularly fast. He wasn't excessively strong. He was just this amalgam of brazen skill and deep imagination. And, perhaps most amazing of all, we sometimes ran into him on the streets.

Now, it wasn't unusual for us to see Cork hurlers and footballers in our daily lives but it was still always a bit of a thrill. Johnny Buckley, the moustachioed wingback/forward from Glen Rovers, used to collect insurance payments in our neighbourhood, and patiently entertain our entreaties that he'd kick a ball with us. Scarcely a day went by when Gerald McCarthy, holder of a mere five All-Irelands, didn't zoom along Clashduv Road at the wheel of his van on the way to his house in nearby Summerstown. These became such quotidian occurrences though that they lost their lustre after a while.

Seeing Jimmy though was always an event. A couple of days after he gave a master class in the 1985 Munster hurling final against Tipperary, I stood behind him in the queue at Jackie Lennox's fish and chip shop on Bandon Road. I was fourteen by then, desperately trying to affect an air of cool in everything I did. But on that occasion I just stared and stared at him as he lined up with the rest of us plebs to place his order. This must have been what it would have been like to see Clark Kent queuing at a hot dog stand outside the Daily Planet hours after saving the world.

Jimmy was the man through whom we eventually learned the meaning of the word charisma. Whatever that is, we were constantly assured he had it. And all we knew was that we wanted it too. We wanted to try to be like him. He walked before matches with the hurley pressed against his side, perfectly horizontal and balanced. So we did too. It was good that we could successfully ape him in that regard because so much about the rest of his work on the field was beyond us mere mortals.

On an August afternoon in 1983, my parents and I were sitting on the couch, watching the All-Ireland hurling semi-final between Cork and Galway when he scored 'the goal'. For that is how it was known from that point on. The denouement of the score does not do it justice. Dermot McCurtain handpassed to John Fenton in the middle of the field. He then fired the ball in around about head height towards where Jimmy was being closely marked by Conor Hayes on the edge of the square. The Galway full-back was a couple of steps ahead, playing him from the front, doing everything a defender is taught to do. Better-placed than his man, Hayes went up to block, at which point Jimmy's stick came across and somehow, somewhere between good timing and genius, managed in a flash to direct the ball to the back of the net.

'The slow motion won't even slow it down,' shrieked Michael O'Hehir.

The most amazing thing about the greatest hurling highlight of my life is that the ball moved too fast for any camera to properly pick up its path. That we couldn't quite discern the trajectory mattered not a jot. In fact, it possibly made it more wondrous and compelling. We saw the ball leave Fenton's hurley and the rest we played and replayed in our minds a thousand times without quite figuring it out, a sporting Zapruder film that never quite makes sense yet continues to awe.

As much as the goal itself, I remember the morning after. Eddie O'Sullivan, who was dating and later married my mother's youngest sister Christine, called to our house. He had the largest afro this side of 1970s Harlem, a wonderful singing voice and a generous spirit. He invited me to accompany him in his John Player van as he delivered cigarettes to shops and pubs all over West Cork. At every stop we made, in a part of the county hardly synonymous with hurling, shopkeepers and publicans and their customers were talking about it. About Jimmy. About the greatness of the moment.

'Did ye see the goal?' An old woman in a tiny corner store in Bantry had the same sparkle in her eyes as I did as we discussed it.

'Do you think he meant it?' asked one curmudgeon from a bar stool in Clonakilty.

'Of course he meant it,' said Eddie. 'That's Jimmy all out.'

Jimmy all out.

EIGHT

Moving Pictures

One Tuesday night in the winter of 1980, we had that most exciting of events. A stranger calling to our house after dark. By that point, see, I prided myself on being able to identify all regular visitors by the shape they made through the frosted glass of the front door. This was a skill that I'd developed over time since, as the youngest, it had become my job to answer the door. In fact, it had become my job to do just about every chore possible.

I had to get coal from the bunker in the gloomy backyard when the fire started to wane, an especially thankless job in the absence of any light out there. I had to run to the kitchen to turn on the kettle a minute before the break in *Quicksilver*, the quiz show where contestants won pennies and all of us learned the catchphrase 'Stop the lights!'. I had to go fetch my sisters from their friends' houses. I had to go find Tom on the street. Basically, I was Dobby the house elf.

This is how I found myself opening the door that particular evening to an excessively large man in square glasses, wearing a leather coat and carrying a suitcase. He looked like an intimidating cross between some long-lost relative who'd just touched down at Cork Airport and a grim-faced assassin sent to kill us all by the mob.

'Is your father in, boy?' he asked in a deep voice that suited his scary persona.

The impromptu arrival of a stranger like this was so thrilling I had no training in what to do next. I'd seen well brought up English kids on television shows ask polite questions like 'Who will I say is calling?' but that seemed a little too much Little Lord Fauntleroy for Togher.

'I'll get him now,' I squeaked.

My father rose from the chair, unhappy, irritated at being disturbed from his throne and his evening's viewing. Curious as to what might happen next, I took a position just inside the living room door so I could observe what was sure to be a fascinating encounter through the jamb. There was no need. The stranger was immediately invited in. Not into the hallway where most visitors were usually quarantined because my mother was obsessed with them being somewhat disturbed by 'the state of the room'. No, this fellow was granted instant access to the inner sanctum. That was when I knew something was up. The stranger in our midst had to be pretty special to be afforded this sort of privilege.

It was turning out to be quite the exciting Tuesday night.

The large man took off his leather coat and started to unstrap his briefcase. At which point we all gasped and realised who he was and why he had come. The inside of it was lined very neatly with VHS video cassettes. Not real ones. Not ones with actual covers. These were copies and the only thing identifying the films they contained were the names scrawled in black marker along the edge. The whiff of illegality about the whole business only added to our excitement.

Several weeks earlier, one of my uncles had convinced my parents to buy a Grundig VHS video recorder from him. It was so hefty, thick and square that it needed two adults to carry it into the front room and to place it beneath the television. Then it took them an hour or so of finagling wires, cursing under their breath and fiddling with tuners before it actually worked.

We looked at this silver and black machine in awe and wonder, a bunch of petrified earthlings gazing upon a superior alien life form that had come from a faraway galaxy to rule their lives.

'Don't touch it,' we were warned repeatedly.

As if we would have dared. This was a collection of buttons and technology and tuners that, as my father kept saying, looked capable of launching a rocket into space.

Part of the initial purchase involved one free movie, a pirate copy of *Dog Day Afternoon*. The classic bank caper featuring Al Pacino and John Cazale was deemed too mature (my dad's phrase) for us. This meant the video recorder we'd heard so much about was nothing more than a piece of extremely hi-tech, modern furniture for those first few weeks. This made my father's initial declaration that 'It'll be like having the pictures in the house!' ring a tad hollow.

'Don't worry,' said my uncle, 'there'll be a fella calling one of these Tuesday nights.'

This was how business was done. A succession of people came to our door each week, delivering goods and/or collecting money. None of them ever had actual names. They were just known by the nature of the business involved. For instance, the *Echo* boy delivered the evening paper. But be was only one of the cast of regulars. There was also the rent man, the insurance man, the egg man, the coalman, the vegetable man. When the time of their appointed visit loomed, my mother would have the exact change ready on the hall-table to speed them on their way.

Several Tuesday nights passed without any sign of the character we would henceforth know as 'the video man'. Now, finally, he had arrived and was flaunting his wares. In the absence of a cover containing a blurb about the film, he offered his own personal critique in a unique shorthand.

'*Kramer vs Kramer*. About a divorce. Sad. Women love it.'

'*Death Wish*. Charles Bronson killing bad guys. Very good.'

'*Rocky*. Boxing. Brilliant.'

Those were the first three he offered. Those were the first three we rented that week, divided neatly along age and gender lines. One for my mother and the girls. One for my father. One for the boys.

'I'll see you next Tuesday,' said video man, putting on his impressively long leather coat. The moment he left, we all started squabbling about who should get to watch what first.

We'd heard about Rocky but had never seen it. Until now. We were allowed to stay up late to watch in its entirety. A terrible idea. Our adrenalin was pumping at the end, a condition not helped by the fact we pushed the couch back to create a ring so we could re-enact the fight between Rocky Balboa (hurrah!) and Apollo Creed (boo! hiss!). We watched it every day for the next seven days and then we begged my father to rent it again.

'Why would you want to rent something ye've already seen?' he asked.

It was a rhetorical question. He knew the answer. I was moved. I was inspired. I was going to be the next heavyweight champion of the world. Rocky had just given me the template. Sure, I may not have had the seventy-two steps of the Philadelphia Museum of Art to run up. But I had the ability to improvise in and around the house.

'Will you stop that?' roared my mother, standing at the bottom of the stairs.

'Why?' I asked, from the landing to which I'd just sprinted for the twenty-fifth time in a row – of course I was counting.

'You'll break the bloody stairs!'

This was the kind of strange reasoning behind a lot of my mother's domestic rules. How could I, a scrawny nine-year-old boy, barely tipping the scales at four stone, break the bloody stairs? The weight of my footfalls, cushioned by thick carpet too, was hardly going to crack the steps. Of course, there was no reasoning with her on that particular score. So I tramped defeated to my bedroom, lamenting the fact that a difficult mother was one obstacle Balboa never had to navigate on his way to the title.

From repeated watching of the video, my obsession grew to an extent that decades later I cannot say the name Adrian without closing my eyes and shouting Stallone-like 'Adriannnnn!' For weeks after the video came in the house, I saw echoes of it everywhere. When I walked through the English Market with my mother, I stared longingly at the carcasses of the dead cows that hung behind many of the butchers' stalls. All I needed was somebody to allow me in there at night, after the customers had gone home, so I could work on my punches and simultaneously tenderise the meat they sold. Just like Rocky did.

When I apprised my mother of this plan, she was as unsupportive as ever.

'There's a want in you boy,' she said, 'a want.'

She was not wrong. My next step in my ongoing effort to emulate Rocky was to improve my diet. I knew I had to put on weight if I was ever going to make it as a heavyweight so I decided there was nothing for it but to start quaffing the yolks of raw eggs. There was a couple of problems with this plan. I hated eggs. With a passion. The smell of them cooking made me nauseous. Never mind the taste.

One evening when everybody else was watching *Hart to Hart*, I snuck into the kitchen, cracked open two eggs and poured them into an empty Murphy's pint glass. I was well-prepared. Earlier that day, I'd stolen a wooden clothes peg from the clothes line in the back garden that I now placed over my nose. Then, bold as brass and twice as stupid, I decided to go for it. I tasted nothing but slime going down my throat and appeared to have pulled it off. I breathed out. Relieved. I took the peg off and started rubbing my nose where it now hurt. And then it hit me. Somewhere in my stomach the arrival of the eggs prompted a sort of mutiny. I was halfway towards the back door when I threw up all over the floor.

My mother came through from the living room with the speed of Creed. After the clean-up operation, Rocky was briefly banned until I came to my senses.

In the absence of actually watching it I merely recited lines of the dialogue to myself.

'Women weaken legs!' I'd say this in my best Mickey accent, a pre-pubescent Cork boy channeling his inner Burgess Meredith. I loved that line. I didn't quite know what it meant, but I know I hated girls too.

There was another soliloquy I liked to recite into the mirror in the bathroom.

'What about my prime, Mick? At least you had a prime! I had no prime. I had nothin'!'

To me, this was eloquence itself. A couple of years down the line, a teacher in Coláiste an Spioraid Naoimh made us watch *On The Waterfront* and I discovered the lyrical writing of Budd Schulberg and the magic of Brando delivering 'I coulda been a contender.' At nine though, Stallone was far simpler and superior. He had me in his maw. *Rocky II* deepened the addiction and then there came the third instalment, the first of the series that I saw on the big screen, at the Capitol cinema on the Grand Parade.

The artistic merits of the film didn't concern me as much as the cultural fusion that took place. Aside from Hulk Hogan, whose cameo offered an awful preview of the WWF (later WWE) wrestling that soon blighted the imaginations and destroyed some of the brightest minds of our generation, there was Mr T as Clubber Lang. Again, he was to loom large in our lives for the ensuing few years on *The A-Team*, that magnificent show where nobody ever seemed to die in the high-powered shoot-outs and explosions that were standard fare in every episode.

Most of all though, *Rocky III* gave us 'Eye of the Tiger', the Survivor song. Even now the sound of the opening riff – dun… dun, dun, dun… dun, dun, dun… – is enough to get the blood pumping, several chords before I even hear Dave Bickler's voice intoning, 'Risin' up, back on the streets, did my time, took my chances…'

I had never done any time but that didn't matter. Myself and all my friends were searching for the eye of the tiger. The closest we may have come to finding it was when headbanging to this song at Saturday night teen discos in Bishopstown GAA club a few years later.

On 3 May 1980 there was a small item on the news pages of my copy of *SHOOT!* magazine that caught my eye. It was the

headline 'Ipswich co-star Michael Caine'. I knew the whole Ipswich Town team. I'd never heard of him. I think I knew there was an actor of that name but what was he doing playing for Ipswich? The answer, of course, was that he wasn't. The story centred on how Hollywood had finally decided to make a proper soccer movie. The entire Ipswich squad, it seemed, had been signed up to spend part of their summer shooting a film in Hungary with the famed American director John Huston. Never heard of him either but apparently he was a big, big deal.

'It's a tight schedule but there should be a few laughs,' said Kevin Beattie. 'I never thought of myself looking like Michael Caine but after this I might ask for a transfer to Hollywood!'

Aside from the eminently quotable Beattie, uber-moustachioed John Wark and the rest of Bobby Robson's team that never won the league title their consistency deserved, the cast included Caine, Sylvester Stallone and Pelé. This was beyond my wildest dreams. A movie featuring Rocky and Pelé. The cinematic stars had aligned in my favour.

A contingent from Mr Healy's fifth class went to the Capitol to watch *Escape to Victory* when it eventually came out. A contingent from Mr Healy's fifth class left the cinema convinced they had just seen the greatest war film ever made. Sure, other generations might have prized *Patton* or *The Guns of Navarone* or even *The Great Escape*. Decent productions all. None had anything on this meisterwerk in which a group of Allied prisoners of war are persuaded to play an exhibition match against a German team.

To explain our warped judgement, it's necessary to understand we were a generation who thought *Baa Baa Black Sheep*, a short-lived sitcom involving fighter pilots wisecracking their way around the Pacific Ocean during World War II, was also classic. Cineastes we were not.

Preparations for the fixture between the Germans and the Allied prisoners are complicated by various storylines. The Nazis are using the event for propaganda purposes and the prison escape committee want to concoct some sort of plan to strike a blow back. The latter plot culminates in Robert Hatch (Stallone) having to be drafted into the team at the last minute so he can escape. The problem is that he's in solitary confinement (after a previous escape, do keep up!) so the only way the Germans will let him out is if the team has no other goalkeeping option.

'I won't even see the game will I,' says Kevin O'Callaghan as Tony Lewis, moments before he volunteers to get his arm broken so that Hatch can come in as his replacement.

This was extremely confusing. O'Callaghan was usually a flying winger and an Irish international. Here, he was a goalie, speaking in a perfect London accent.

'Dad, I thought Kevin O'Callaghan was Irish?' I asked.

'Sshhhh. He's English-Irish.'

'Like the dictionary Tom has?'

'No, like your cousins over in Birmingham,' he replied. 'They're us but they talk different.'

After a brutal first half in which a combination of dodgy refereeing and horrendous fouling has helped the Germans to a 4–1 lead, the Allies retire to the dressing-room. Not just to lick their wounds but to make good their escape. Moments later, the French resistance come tunnelling in through the team bath and offer them the chance to run for freedom. And this is the pivotal moment where a good movie becomes great.

Many of the players are already in the sewers below what is supposed to be the Colombes Stadium in Paris when a debate breaks out about whether they are doing the right thing. Some want to stay and try to make a comeback. In a deliciously ludicrous twist, the competitive spirit of the footballers they used to be over-rides the inclinations of the soldiers they now are.

'If we run now we lose more than a game,' says Luis Fernandez (Pelé), persuading Hatch that playing with honour is apparently worth more than the chance to be liberated.

Hatch is convinced. Pelé's words perhaps carry extra weight because he's pinning his left arm to his side, protecting ribs damaged in a savage assault in the first half. That spirit of defiance leads to the greatest moment in the history of soccer cinema – not a tough category admittedly.

'I must play,' says Fernandez, rising from the bench with four minutes remaining in the match and the Allies having pegged the score back to 4–3.

With the ball at his feet, Fernandez holds off the German Number 4, Baumann (played by Werner Roth, a Yugoslav-born American and former New York Cosmos team-mate of Pelé's). After taking several punches to the chest before nutmegging Baumann, he almost stumbles in the act of finally wriggling free. Somehow he stays upright before knocking the ball out to Terry Brady (Bobby Moore) wide on the right. Brady unfurls a delightful cross and then it happens…

Left arm still pinned to his chest, Fernandez rises and executes the perfect overhead kick to make it 4–4. While legend has it that Pelé only needed one take to pull it off, the goal was also John Huston's finest hour.

Yes, I'm aware purists reckon his finest cinematic achievements were *The Maltese Falcon* or *The African Queen*. I'm sorry. I disagree. I reckon it was his decision to break with convention and to show a slow motion replay of Pelé's overhead kick. It's one thing getting the best out of Humphrey Bogart in *The Treasure of the Sierra Madre*, it's quite another capturing the poetry of one-armed Pelé in full flight. Not to mention appreciating the genius of it enough to show it twice.

An earlier slo-mo shot of Carlos Rey (Ossie Ardiles) rainbowing the ball over an on-rushing German player offers further proof that Huston deserved some sort of award for his work on this movie. He knew what his audience wanted. He knew how to make a bunch of ten- and eleven-year-old boys ooh and aah. He died not long after, probably never realising how much he inspired a kid in Togher to spend hours trying and failing to master the Ardiles move.

Of course, the drama wasn't over. There was still time for a German counter. In the final minute of the game, Ardiles is judged to have fouled Baumann inside the box and the ref points to the spot. I had a few problems with this scene. I saw a lot of Ardiles with Argentina and with Tottenham, and I never remember him spending any time in his own box. I can recall him picking out any number of visionary passes and scoring a few too on *Match of the Day*. When it comes to images of him tackling at all, never mind scything down somebody, the highlight reel is completely blank.

'At the end of the game, they've resorted to fouling,' says the pro-German commentator.

Whatever about the initial contact, more than one of the Allies could have subsequently been sent off for jostling and manhandling both the ref and the linesman in the immediate aftermath of the penalty award. Amid the mayhem though, the crowd are so enflamed by the injustice that they start into the opening bars of 'La Marseillaise'. A scene that made our pre-pubescent hearts beat quicker. Then Stallone walks out to the spot to try to intimidate Baumman as he prepares to take the kick.

I loved that scene. Well at least until I later discovered it was a hastily rewritten add-on because Stallone, as the most box office name, had insisted his character Hatch should score the winning goal. When it was explained to him that this was kind of stretching the bounds of credulity, a compromise had to be found. Hence the penalty. In that same article, it was also reported that the American went all Hollywood on set, having his own chair that nobody else was allowed to sit in. And, rather than hanging with the rest of the cast at weekends, he flew to Paris to party. Even if that was Rocky's prerogative, it shattered my illusions about the multinational dream team of which he'd been such a crucial part.

'Come on 'atch!' shouts Sid Harmor (Mike Summerbee) as the tension builds for the penalty. 'Come on!'

Diving to his left, grimacing like Balboa about to absorb a right cross to the chin, Hatch grabs Baumann's rather tentative effort. Up in the stands, the German officer, Major Karl Von Steiner (Max von Sydow), rises to applaud. He had to. He was, just like us, at the end of it all, still a fan of the game.

There's a moment where Hatch runs into the ensuing celebration and thunders into Pelé's left side, lifting him up into the air. For a man with cracked ribs in that very location, it must have caused excruciating pain, but Fernandez is beaming with delight, oblivious to the agony. Maybe historic comebacks do that to a body.

By then the crowd are chanting 'Victoire! Victoire!' The scoreline might have read 4–4 but this was a triumph of the spirit. It was also a game and a movie that contained everything we loved. Eight goals. The kind of scoreline we dreamed of on *Match of the Day* highlights that always ended 1–1. Drama. Controversy. Ridiculously audacious tricks. And, then, of course, an escape as the crowd rushed the field after the penalty.

The fact so many of the gleeful supporters swarming all over the Allied players are dressed like Hungarians from the 1980s and not Parisiens in Vichy France didn't bother us a jot. In the cinema that day, we were too busy cheering at them as they threw overcoats and caps onto the escaping footballers and then pushed through the gates where the armed German guards showed a marked reluctance to offer any resistance at all! They were, like us, probably too intoxicated by what they had just seen to care.

It was exactly one mile from our house to my grandmother's on McDonagh Road in Ballyphehane. My mother's devotion to her own mother meant that we visited there almost every single night of my childhood, whether we liked it or not. Mostly, we liked it because her house was a busy and chaotic place, teeming with personalities and suffused with drama. While my younger uncles and aunts still lived under her roof there was constant traffic, between them and the people they were dating, and the ensuing sideshows were inevitably entertaining. Not to mention there was always a chance one of them might dispatch me up to Carroll's shop on Kilreendowney Avenue for cigarettes.

'Ten John Player Blue please,' I would ask, pound note in hand.

'Who are they for, boy?' Mary at the till would counter.

'My uncle,' I replied hoping, Mary wouldn't interrogate my nine-year-old self any further.

'Who's your uncle?'

'Tommy Morrissey.'

'Are you one of the Morrisseys?'

'Yes.'

'Are you Sheila's or Theresa's?'

'Theresa's.'

'Oh right.' Her debriefing complete. 'Grand, so.' She handed me the box and the change I knew was bound to be soon mine.

One typical evening in McDonagh Road, my future Uncle Eddie spotted that I was bored senseless by whatever peace treaty my mother was negotiating between her warring younger siblings in the box room.

'Did you ever see *Giants of Brazil*?'

'No.'

'Get your jacket.'

'Taking Dave up to my mam's to show him a film,' he shouted as we headed out.

Moments later we were walking in the door of his family home in nearby Loreto Park. Two of his brothers were watching television when we walked in and they appeared unmoved when he announced he was putting on *Giants of Brazil* for the young fella. They had no problem with the sudden change in the scheduled programming, which made me even more excited about what was in prospect.

It didn't start promisingly though. It was all in black and white and that just reminded me of bored Sunday afternoons at home. Then there was footage of babies kicking balls around parks, shirtless men playing barefoot on mud patches and grainy sepia-tinted footage of the 1938 and 1950 World Cups. Sure, the crowd shots were impressive, a stadium full of 150,000 fans was quite the sight, but I was still wondering what all the fuss was about.

Then there appeared Garrincha, the little bird who had been crippled from boyhood. I saw a couple of his dribbles and suddenly I started to understand. And that was only the warm-up act for the arrival of Pelé. Like Christy Ring, I knew of Pelé's greatness from my father and other grown-ups. His genius was an article of faith. Yet, slight problem, I'd never seen any of him on television. Until now.

Here he was in all his glory, scoring for Brazil and Santos. All kinds of goals too. Shots from outside the box, tap-ins at the end of mazy runs, chips and even one penalty, significant because it marked the 1000th goal of his career! He celebrated by running into the net and kissing the ball.

If those were enough to bring me to the edge of the couch, the lowlight reel showing the horrendous fouls committed against him by opponents kept me there. One miscreant, and this stood out because I had most certainly never seen it on *Match of the Day* or *Sports Stadium*, tried to pull him back by the shorts and almost de-pantsed him.

Then there was the rest of the supporting cast at his first World Cup, Dida, Vava, Gilmar and, of course, Garrincha. The narrator recited the names with a poetic flourish to match the lyricism of the scenes of their genius on the way to victory in Chile. Then, in one of several bizarre production decisions, there followed a montage of savage and brutal fouls from what, Eddie explained to me, was Brazilian club football.

Still, there was stuff to fire the imagination of any child, cameos of wonder that made you want to run out onto a field right then and play. Against Bulgaria, Garrincha struck a free-kick with the outside of his right boot that swerved inside the wall on its way to the top corner as the goalie dived in vain. It defied physics the way it bent air en route. We stopped and rewound a dozen times to savour the bizarre trajectory. Quite an accolade given that stopping and rewinding meant somebody lying on the floor next to the machine and manually pressing the required buttons.

That goal was in 1966, a year, I now learned, when Pelé had been the victim of a brutal takedown by Portugal's João Morais. It was an assault in two acts. When Pelé extricated himself from the first heavy tackle, Morais kept up the pursuit, this time scything him down properly, ending his and, effectively, Brazil's interest in the tournament. To make matters worse, the ref that failed to send the Portuguese player off was an Englishman by the name of George McCabe.

'That would be a red in Ballyphehane Park,' said Eddie.

His brothers agreed. So I did too.

The controversial decision by McCabe to allow Morais stay on the field was followed by another bizarre interlude, this time showing clips of animated, presumably Brazilian referees gesticulating, wagging fingers and shuffling gracelessly around pitches, their every gesture set to elevator music. At times the film was frankly strange. All the magic punctuated by these odd montages of over the top tackles, wild kicks, stamps, and outbreaks of fisticuffs that were somewhat out of kilter with the upbeat soft jazz backing track.

The best bit, for me, was a game that degenerated into a running battle between the subs and mentors of one team and the players of another. That we didn't know the teams involved, or weren't told, scarcely mattered. All we cared about was the fact that here was a chase scene like something from the end credits of *Benny Hill.*

Eventually, Eddie ensured that a pirated copy of *Giants of Brazil* made its way into our burgeoning video collection at home and it was soon almost worn out from being played and replayed. It possibly didn't help that we were constantly rewinding to scenes we loved. Apart from the various wonder goals, we paused again and again at an incident where two cops are strong-arming a hooligan off the field. The peculiar thrill was that, as they walk, one of the policemen is repeatedly hitting the miscreant sneaky blows behind his back with his truncheon, not realising there's a camera trained on him. We were easily amused.

Through this repeated watching, I became obsessed with a section showing footage of the Brazilians training for the 1970 World Cup. Aside from the usual running and shooting drills, they seemed to be doing a lot of innovative routines. These involved players contorting their bodies in ways we never did at training with Summerstown United. One that caught my eye involved players sitting with their backs to each other, twisting and turning, passing a ball back and forth with their hands. Core work, it would probably be called today.

Bereft of a training partner, I used to improvise this procedure on the bedroom floor. Placing the ball behind me on the grass, well, carpet, I coiled my torso to pick it up then transferred it to the other side and repeated like a hundred times. If it was good enough for Tostão, Jairzinho and Rivellino, it was good enough for me, although I did wonder whether it made their tummies hurt like mine did. Or if they were sometimes interrupted in their routines by an older brother walking in, scoffing and telling them they were acting the gowl.

An amazing thing happens in *Giants of Brazil* during the build-up to the 1970 World Cup: the film moves from black and white to technicolour. Suddenly, I saw Brazil wearing that glorious yellow, a shirt myself and a million other boys started to worship in earnest in the summer of 1982. That was when we fell in love with Zico, Sócrates and Éder, the heirs to the great tradition. That they never won a World Cup didn't affect their vaunted place in our affections. They were our own Pelé, Tostão and Garrincha.

'Wait now, wait now,' said Eddie, prepping me for Brazil versus England in Guadalajara. Suddenly, Gordon Banks was diving to his right, palming away Pelé's header for *that* save. Then there was Jairzinho's goal from a delightful Pelé pass and Jeff Astle's equally memorable miss. Eventually I knew these plays down to the minutest detail – but never tired of watching them.

How could I? Here was Pelé in the semi-final selling the famous dummy to Ladislao Mazurkiewicz in the Uruguayan goal. That he subsequently missed didn't bother me or any of us in the slightest. The audacity of the enterprise imprinted itself on our brains in a way that so many goals never did. Indeed, it may be the most memorable moment in the film because Carlos Alberto's goal in the final, which should be the highlight, isn't quite up to the job. Not in this edition.

As was his duty during my initial viewing, Eddie told me it was the greatest goal ever scored. His brothers concurred. It was obvious even to ten-year-old me that it was a fine goal, the nonchalance of Pelé's no-look pass marking it out as different. Yet a part of me was not that impressed. I'd seen Glenn Hoddle score better, more spectacular strikes. Many times.

It was only years later that I realised why I was so underwhelmed. The version of the goal that is on *Giants of Brazil* is truncated and cuts out almost all the build-up. Nearly a decade passed until I saw the complete version, with Tostão tracking back to win the initial ball, Clodoaldo dribbling past four Italians, Pelé and Gérson knocking the ball about, and Rivellino feeding Jairzinho, who cuts in from the left towards the box.

In a move that showcases perhaps a frightening lack of appreciation for the game, the director only shows the move from the moment Jairzinho starts to sidle in from the wing. This would be like showing an edit of *Saving Private Ryan* with the opening scenes on Omaha Beach cut out. And yet, notwithstanding that drastic error of judgement, to my ten-year-old mind, this was the greatest sports documentary I'd ever seen. Of course, it was also the first, and for a long time, the only sports documentary I'd ever seen.

NINE

Have Boots, Will Travel

I got my first pair of soccer boots at age seven. They were hand-me-downs. Not just ordinary hand-me-downs, these were heirlooms that came replete with an entertaining backstory and an illustrious heritage. According to my mother, they had belonged briefly to Tom, even if I had no memory of him ever wearing them. And before that, she said they had been worn by her own younger brothers, my uncles Ger and Tommy. All three of the previous owners who had played in the boots before me then were, in her parlance, 'known all over Cork as grand players'. With these on my feet, the implication was that I would be too. I bought into my mother's belief that I was next in line to the throne of greatness. She was equal parts mother and fledgling sports psychologist.

The boots were certainly unique. Apart from various other attributes, they were white. In a time before football footwear turned gaudily technicolour, they stood out among all the black. When I say they were white, of course, I mean they began life that colour but the ravages of use had made them more of a watery beige by the time they came into my possession. No matter. They were still louder than any other pair on the field. Every field.

Dodgy colour aside, they also had black moulded soles, four studs at the back, seven at the front, and, even more strangely, the phrase 'Made in England' stamped in between. Fashioned from the type of hard industrial and damn near indestructible plastic that environmental scientists estimate will take a thousand years to biodegrade, they were stiff and heavy. In the spirit of the time, this, ahem, firmness to the touch was sold to me as a positive. It would, my brother told me, perhaps prompted by our mother, allow me to hit the ball way harder than everybody else. That sounded logical enough to my seven-year-old brain.

They had other virtues too. Steve Heighway's autograph, barely visible in gold ink, was written on the outside of the upper, just beneath a crest. Not his actual autograph, of course, but one that had been embossed there by a machine in a factory. Again, the fact my boots were personally endorsed by the moustachioed Liverpool and Ireland winger was used to convince me of their merits. This sales pitch worked too.

I hated Liverpool, but I knew Heighway's name. I'd seen him on *Match of the Day* a few times and the fact he played for Ireland impressed me too. Not that it mattered either way. I had no choice. These were the boots I was given. These were the boots that were available. These were the boots I would wear. Regardless.

This much was hammered home to me when I tried them on. They were too big. Way too big. They were size 2 when I was still struggling to fill out a child's size 12 shoe. That's a lot of room for growth. No problem. An *Evening Echo* was soon being torn apart and inserted into the toe of each boot. Another fitting.

Slightly better this time but still more than a little spacious. Fret not. Another pair of football socks were sourced upstairs. With two pairs on, the fit was quite snug, according to my mother, who, crucially, wasn't the person wearing them. In actual fact, my toes were still barely reaching the folded-up newsprint – but I knew there was no point in complaining. Instead, I went out the front to sprint up and down the lawn to get the feel of them, then I started trying to solo a punctured plastic soccer ball toe to hand – a skill more difficult to pull off than it sounds.

The new, old boots were needed for my debut as a Gaelic footballer. For two years I had traipsed after Tom as he played for a team with the unwieldy name of Glasheen/Wilton in the street leagues at Bishopstown GAA club. Now, I was finally old enough to make my bow in that competition. It was Under-10 but the team was run by Mr Healy from our school, and he knew that what I lacked for in size and talent I would make up for with enthusiasm. Not to mention that they were always struggling to field fifteen players anyway and he knew I'd turn up.

The squad convened on Sunday mornings at the bottom of the school hill. I loved every part of the ritual. I walked up the road on my own, Gola gear bag slung over my shoulder, barely looking seven but attempting to swagger like I was seventeen. Once enough players sauntered along, we were piled into two cars, one driven by Mr Healy, the other by whichever parent had enlisted to help us. Off we went.

For me, this was an essential part of the glamour of getting involved. Travelling in strange cars to a match. Like a real player. On a real team. There was a buzz too about getting togged out in an actual dressing-room, the air thick with the smell of toe-jam, flecks of caked mud pockmarking the floor.

The details were important because at last I was getting my chance.

'Top of the left,' said Mr Healy when he put his hands on my shoulders.

'Top of the left,' I repeated back to him, as if trying to reassure us both.

I put on the hairy black shirt my brother had worn the previous two seasons and I felt fantastic. At least until I looked around and noticed the footwear of my team-mates. None of their boots were mostly beige or any diluted variation of white. All of them were wearing the type of brands that cluttered up the ad section of *SHOOT!*: Adidas, Puma, Gola. Still, nobody else was flaunting a Steve Heighway signature and, literally, following in the footsteps of their family. That thought consoled me at least until disaster struck.

As we walked from the dressing-room to the field one of the older kids noticed my distinctive footwear and immediately christened me 'Little Boots'. They weren't little, I wanted to shout but didn't. They are size 2. It's just the colour makes them look smaller. I should have spoke out when I had the chance. It took me two years to shake off that name.

I didn't touch the ball much that first season. Whenever it came near me I was jostled and bustled out of the way by bigger, faster, hell I'll admit it, better kids. I wasn't unduly bothered. After watching from the sidelines for so long, it was a thrill just to be involved. The low-point of the season came when a behemoth full-back from The Rise/Halldene team trod on my left foot. The hard plastic protected me from injury but his studs tore one of the eyelets. I didn't get a look at the culprit. I suspect from the damage that he was wearing those ankle-high rugby boots when he committed the crime. Those were standard-issue weapons for full-backs of that era.

Ripping through this plastic was some achievement though. The Incredible Hulk himself would have struggled to tear this material with his bare hands. After the initial panic upon reviewing the tear, I began to wonder whether there might be an upside to this incident. Could this lead to me being bought a new pair, perhaps even a pair with three stylish stripes down each side like my brother now wore? As if. My mother was of the make and mend generation. She picked up the boot when I got home, surveyed the vandalism and nodded her head in a way that showed this was not going to be an issue.

'I can fix this,' she said. And my heart sank.

She was soon foraging in the drawers of the stand-up Singer sewing machine where she kept an assortment of needles and threads for every clothing emergency. From that treasure trove she produced a leather thread and announced casually that she would stich the broken eyelet back together. No problem. No fuss. And that's what she did. Right then. As I watched her.

With the steady hand of a surgeon, she threaded the needle through the surface of the upper and then repeated the action again from a higher point. Evincing all the expertise gained in her years in the Sunbeam factory, she built a bridge of leather binding together the two halves that had been torn apart. It was a dexterous feat of imagination and skill. She was a seamstress. She was a magician.

'There you go, boy, good as new,' she said, handing it to me as I faked a smile.

I wore them for two more years, taking out a little bit of the newspaper padding every few months, an action which miraculously improved my touch. Somewhere along the way I perfected the art of being a sneaky-liner corner-forward and, as the older boys graduated out of street leagues to more serious fare, I eventually even lost the 'Little Boots' moniker. The name had to go. Nobody could call me that, especially when I was finally allowed to discard my white Steve Heighways and started to wear a pair of brand-spanking new Adidas Hansi Müllers.

They weren't Tom's. They weren't even passed on by my uncles. Well, in actual fact, they were. Kind of. When my parents finally acknowledged that my toes were hurting so bad after every match that it was time to retire the Heighways (still remarkably intact), they gave me rather strange instructions. I was told to go to Wilton Shopping Centre to try on a pair of Hansi Müllers and to find the size that fit me.

It should be pointed out that Hansi Mullers were chosen not because of my admiration for the German international. In actual fact, I had just a vague memory of him impressing in the 1980 European Championships. I was instructed to try on his brand because they were cheaper than the other Adidas model, the Franz Beckenbauers.

In my innocence, I thought the fitting was a prelude to one of my parents then accompanying me to purchase the pair. Nope, the scheme was much more labyrinthine than that. Once I ascertained that I was now a size 3, my mother said, 'Okay, boy, leave it with me.'

'When are we going to go get them?

She seemed puzzled.

'Going to get them? We aren't going to get them.'

'But you told me to try them on?'

'Oh, yeah, your uncle knows a fella working in the Adidas factory in Ballyphehane, and he'll put in the order with his friend and then he'll deliver them.'

Having my boots stolen to order wasn't what I envisaged but she promised they would arrive. And two weeks later they did. My uncle pulled up and there in the back seat of his car in a bright-blue coloured box were my Hansi Müllers. These were the real deal all right. They were so impossibly soft I kept pressing my fingers into them. Then, using the wrench that came with the box, I spent a happy hour at the kitchen table that night, just screwing the studs in and out, like a Formula One crew man practising taking off the tyres until he has it down to an art.

Every time I took the field in those Hansi Müllers, and every boots I owned thereafter, they were invariably spotless and clean. Not due to my diligence but because of my father. He couldn't, as my mother would remind him, hammer in a nail yet he was curiously determined that his boys would always play in boots that were in perfect nick.

'Have you a match tomorrow?'

'Yes.'

'Where are your boots?'

'Out on the back step.' Where I'd left them six or seven days earlier when I returned from my last game.

'Get them for me.'

The remnants of the last pitch they played on were layered into the sole and, if I had left them too near the edge of the porch, they might also be soaked with rain. Grist to his mill.

The cleaning was ritualistic and thorough. He'd walk to the top of the back garden, and slam them together until the hardened muck flew off into the bushes. Then he'd run them under the trickle of a warm tap in the kitchen sink, an action that always annoyed my mother. Once they were damp on the outside, he went at them with a scrubbing brush that fit around his hand, a device he kept under the kitchen sink for this sole purpose.

'Are you watching now?'

I was always watching, but it didn't matter because he never let me do it. He wanted them to be perfect and only he could assure that.

Once they were spotless, there began the search for a couple of old newspapers whose pages he could tear up and stuff inside to soak up the moisture and to ensure the boots kept their shape. Then he'd send me to procure a jar of Vaseline from the bathroom. He'd lavish globs of petroleum jelly onto the uppers and rub it in until it was almost invisible except for the odd trace line and the sticky sheen that the boots now gave off. Finally, they were placed on the remains of the newspapers just inside the back door.

'You're ready to go now.'

And I was. Thanks to him. I always was.

I was thirteen when I developed my first serious crush. The object of my affections was named Michel, and, as is too often the way of relationships at that age, the love was unrequited. It had to be because there were a few serious obstacles blocking our path to true love, not least the distance and the language barrier between us, and the fact he didn't know I existed. Then there was the age difference. He was twenty-seven years old, hailed from France and lived in Turin where he played for Juventus.

For two magical weeks in the early summer of 1984 though, as he bestrode the European Championships, Michel Platini had myself, and most other boys with any passing interest in the game, in his thrall. I didn't want to be with him. I just wanted to be him.

It wasn't just that he led France to an improbable victory and got to hoist the Henri Delaunay trophy above his head, it was the style with which he did so. The way he carried himself. The way he glided rather than ran. The way he caressed the ball with his eloquent right foot, the way he met headers with just enough force to direct them home. Hell, even the way his jersey hung so perfectly on his frame somehow looked different. Classier. With his always slightly unkempt hair, he could have slung the strap of a Fender Stratocaster over his shoulder and fronted an indie band from Liverpool. He was that cool.

With the languid Jean Tigana, the mischievous Alain Giresse and the mercurial and unforgettably-named Didier Six, it was a wonderful supporting cast and a very special French team. But Platini was the heart and soul of the side. Before, during and after every match that RTÉ showed during that tournament, the boys of Clashduv Road could be found strutting their stuff in 'The Bog'. Our own personal field of dreams. Well, not quite.

In the late 1960s, when those visionary city planners had decided to house us all in Togher, one of the only concessions to the need for open space and recreation was an enormous patch of soggy marsh. Historically, the land had always been bog and having used it as the dumping ground for all the debris of their building work in the area over several years, Cork Corporation then left it idle for about a decade.

A sliver of that waste land abutted Clashduv Road and was just grassy and tamable enough to be cut regularly. It became our arena of choice on summer days when it wasn't pockmarked with pools of water, which meant about half of the time. That particular June, of course, we re-imagined it as the fabled Parc des Princes. Every boy on the street gathered there determined to try to emulate our new-found heroes like Preben Elkjær, Michael Laudrup, just about the entire French team, and, of course, Platini.

There was no age demarcation on that field so the smallest learned to compete with the big kids or, if they were smart, to hang around the fringes of the action, hoping to pilfer the type of goal that would be denounced as 'a sneaky-liner' by jealous opponents. Goalscorers inevitably wheeled away in celebration with an arm in the air and their best beatific smile while, in their well-rehearsed commentator French accent, mouthing the word 'Plateeeneee!' – well, at least I did.

Since it was June darkness didn't fall until well after 10pm. Then the floodlights came on. Or, to be more specific, the street lamps that stretched the length of Clashduv Road. Their sodium-orange glow often allowed us to stretch the game even longer into the night. No school in the morning to bother us.

At any stage, the action might be interrupted by a man sauntering either to or from Flannery's pub at the end of the street. If they were on their way home with a few on board, these cameos usually followed the same pattern. Slightly pie-eyed, these observers would stop to watch. Why? I'm not sure about the scientific evidence but there seems to be something in the male DNA that compels us to always stop to watch boys kicking a ball around. I think we all imagine ourselves somehow to be scouts hoping to unearth the next great wunderkind.

On these nights, we'd pretend not to notice the interlopers, these Corkonian Rabbit Angstroms, while secretly hoping they might be impressed by our brilliance and offer an adult compliment. They almost never did. These interruptions were about them not us, especially if they had a wife or girlfriend on their arm.

Having taken in the action for a few minutes, they'd finally move closer and demand a pass. Upon taking possession, they'd start to try to juggle the ball, a difficult skill to pull off in dress shoes (men still wore actual shoes to the pub in those days) with a few pints on board. Undeterred, they'd persevere while assuring us they had once been quite the prospect. They might even protest that United were on their trail back in the day. We'd offer up our best pained smiles, pretending we hadn't heard it all before and were gullible enough to buy what they were selling.

In a desperate attempt to prove this outrageous assertion, they'd then try some outrageous flick or trick. This was the moment when their inebriated brains discovered they were writing cheques their bodies could no longer cash. Or the balance they once possessed as child prodigies had long since deserted them. Either way, they'd end up on the ground at some point. The happy drunks would wipe the grass from the seats of their good trousers, cackling at their own stupidity. The grumpier ones shuffled off, snorting angrily at their perceived misfortune, a newly-developed limp showing they were now nursing more than a bruised ego.

Every time I think of my childhood trips to the beach in West Cork, there are clouds on the horizon and a whipping breeze that would cut you in half. Every time I think of those matches in 'the bog', the sun is high in the sky in late evening, the air is hot and thick and we all have our shirts off to try to cope with the sapping, humid conditions of tropical Togher.

We played on through that magical twilight until a chorus of mothers eventually stood on the doorsteps to call us home from the creeping darkness. If the game was especially intense, we ignored their shouts until one of them finally might start walking across the road. The sight of a maternal shadow on the move was usually enough to convince us time was officially up. No whistle required.

Since Ireland hadn't qualified for those European Championships, which was the norm back then, we were all free to choose a nation to follow. As soon as Platini started to work his magic, most of us began rooting for France. Glory hunters to a man. Commentators told us the number 10 was carrying the hopes of a nation and by the time France inched past Spain in the final, it looked like the weight of the burden was getting to him.

Even if the last of his nine goals that fortnight barely squirmed under Luis Arconada in the Spanish goal, we didn't care. By then, his legend and his place in our hearts was assured. (Younger readers should note the portly, be-suited Platini who later turned into a UEFA bureaucrat of the most unctuous kind is no relation to this particular deity!)

Back then, in a typically desperate feat of one-upmanship I claimed special kinship with 'Les Bleus'. I'd never been to France but my sister Denise had moved to Paris to work as an au pair the previous year. Under my own convenient reworking of the FIFA rules regarding parentage, birth and eligibility, this somehow qualified me above all my peers to root for her adopted country.

'I'm actually, kind of, sort of, almost French,' I reminded them, regularly. Pathetically.

A school trip to France some years earlier had sparked something in Denise, after which she'd been hell bent on getting back there. Her departure was the cause of much weeping and gnashing of teeth in the house. In the four decades that had passed since my father's sisters, Ellen and Esther, had moved to Birmingham, nobody on either side of the family had emigrated. But, it was okay, Denise assured everybody, it was only for a year. As if. Even at eleven I was smart enough to know from the faraway look in her eyes she had no intention of ever living in Cork again. And wouldn't either for a long time.

Her exile was made more difficult by the fact we didn't have a telephone at home. Very few people on our street did at that time, something that really annoyed teachers and school principals dealing with errant pupils. All official business was conducted in a seriously over-used phone box on Clashduv Estate where clusters of older teenagers gathered each evening to call their beloveds.

The one exception to phone ownership was my mother's friend Mrs Jones who lived down the street. Very kindly, she offered her number as the contact point for Denise.

As a result, dozens of my best games in 'the bog' were interrupted. When my sister phoned from Paris, Mrs Jones strode out on the balcony of her flat, and shouted at me to go fetch my mother. I could be in mid-stride about to score a crucial goal but that didn't matter. I knew time was of the essence. I'd hare home to alert my mother who then shuffled up the street at great pace, often with rollers in her hair and slippers on her feet.

When my friends legitimately complained about a player having the temerity to rush off the field in the middle of a match, I'd protest that my sister was on the phone from France. Actual France! Platini's France. An excuse both glamorous and exotic enough to soon quell any criticism. Of course, every one of these phone calls had the potential to turn soap operatic because I knew my mother would be heartbroken afterwards. Her initial joy at hearing Denise's voice down the phone usually turned to overwhelming melancholy at the growing realisation her eldest daughter was making a new life for herself so very far from home.

After one of those calls during the 1984 European Championships, I ended up sitting in the living room, trying in vain to console my mother while selfishly desperate to get back out to rejoin the action. Between her sobs and sniffles she said, 'She's desperate for someone to come over to visit so I think we'll send you.' Everybody else in the family was working and my ticket would be the cheapest too. Nobody else loved France as much as I did either, I told myself, making me the obvious choice.

I daren't tell my friends on the street for fear it had been the sadness talking and nothing might come of it. But, a few weeks later, the aged Ford Escort was straining up the long hill towards Cork Airport. My excitement had now segued into the queasier side of nervousness. My Dad noticed too.

'Well, you are always reading those adventure books,' he said, 'now you'll have an adventure of your own.'

That didn't make me feel much better. On the plane, the Aer Lingus hostess placed a see-through package around my neck containing my ticket, my passport, a colouring book, stickers and other aviation-related paraphernalia for kids much younger than I. They were treating me like a child. Which is what I was. A skinny, short thirteen-year-old child who'd never flown before, on his way to a foreign country, trying desperately to disguise how scared he was.

Denise worked for a family in the 16th arrondissement. They were so rich that they drank sparkling water out of bottles and ate meals far too sophisticated for my uneducated palate. Part of the problem in this regard was that one of my stated ambitions during my trip was to eat at McDonald's, something we didn't have in Cork. Almost every day, having watched me turn my nose up at every delicacy imaginable, Denise reluctantly brought me to worship at the golden arches on the Champs-Élysées. Like so many culinary tourists to France, I developed a love for the local cuisine or, in my case, Chicken McNuggets.

The whole neighbourhood reeked of class and culture and affluence. A team of men hosed down the streets in the morning and everywhere there were art galleries, foreign embassies and spectacular cars with tinted windows. Parc des Princes was up the road, Roland Garros around the corner. It was head-spinning. Of course, I immediately identified it as just the kind of place where celebrities hung out, an impression copper-fastened by my sister claiming to have met Yannick Noah a few months earlier. I don't know if this was true or just an entertaining yarn she spun to make me even more excited. On the latter score, she succeeded.

Every morning I was dispatched to the local boulangerie to get croissants and to speak bad French to the old lady behind the counter. The moment I pulled back the heavy cast iron gate of the apartment building to set foot on the street I had my eyes peeled. I was convinced I was going to meet Michel Platini on my travels. It was bound to happen. It was fated. If he was in Paris, this was exactly the kind of chic area he'd be hanging in. For nine days in a row, I scanned the faces of passers-by, a very weird Irish kid seeking out his hero.

I was prepared as well. I walked along, rehearsing the conversation in my head, sometimes muttering the words aloud so I could see if I had the pronunciation down.

'Bonjour, Monsieur Platini,' was going to be my opening gambit. I toyed with 'Bonjour Michel' but felt there was an over-familiarity in that approach, I didn't want him to think I was too forward.

'Je m'appelle Davide.' Note: I was going for the full Francophone version of my own name. I had to. I didn't want to confuse him.

'Je suis Irlandais, mais ma sœur elle est Francaise.'

Obviously, this was not technically true but I figured this

might intrigue him enough to continue the conversation before I professed my undying admiration.

'Je suis un grand fan de votre.'

The 'de votre' was a construction beyond the first year French I'd picked up in Coláiste an Spioraid Naoimh. My sister, ever so helpful, added that when I apprised her of my plans.

All my rehearsing and linguistic fine-tuning was in vain. Surprisingly, our paths never crossed during my visit. Platini obviously summered on the Riviera or some place with a beach far from the humidity of Paris in August. Still, I managed, as a consolation prize, to return home with a piece of Platini to treasure forever.

Having spent the day padding around the immense and opulent apartment of the family for whom she worked, we slept in her Spartan quarters, a pokey garret at the top of the building, at night. Denise gave me the bedsprings. She took the mattress onto the floor. Conditions were not ideal and the first time she instructed me in how to jump on and off the Metro without paying, I realised that despite the lavish surroundings, money was tight.

I'd arrived with a bulging envelope of French francs in my bag that my mother had warned me was to be given to Denise without being opened. I obeyed that instruction to the letter. And, thereafter, she paid for everything, including the kitschy keepsakes I picked up for the rest of the family from the African vendors near the Eiffel Tower. With every purchase I was afraid we wouldn't have enough money left for the one thing I desperately wanted for myself. The thing I'd spent weeks dreaming of buying as the ultimate souvenir of my trip. A France shirt. A Platini shirt.

On my very last full day in Paris, using the bizarre ruse that we had to buy my father an expensive tie, my sister took me to a men's clothing store. Not a prospect that excited. At least until I walked through the door. Maybe it was the mood in the summer of 1984 or maybe upscale fashion shops routinely sold soccer kits alongside bespoke suits and shirts. But there it was – in all its glory – on a full-size mannequin in the middle of the store: the blue shirt of Platini.

Just seeing it up close was a thrill. This was a time before every kid wore a soccer shirt on the street. So I was excited just to be able to touch it, to feel the airy Gore-Tex designed to help players sweat (or so I'd read in *SHOOT!*). My sister spoke in her way-too-fast French to the shop assistant. He emerged, in typical Parisian style, with a jersey wrapped in cellophane, folded like a tailored shirt. That was how he presented it to me as well. It was all very formal and kind of magnificent. I went to a tiny changing room at the back of the store to try it on.

Then I emerged. The Adidas logo over my right breast, the strutting cockerel and the FFF of the France Football Federation over my left. I stared at myself longingly in the mirror. It hung on me so perfectly. The distinctive v-neck collar, the thick red stripe and the trio of narrow white lines below somehow made my chest look broader and stronger. But for my nerdy haircut and the fact I looked nothing like the French icon, I could have been Platini's younger brother. Or so I told myself.

I was thirteen, crucially not yet teenage enough to affect disinterest and to conceal my childish glee. My sister, by then gone totally native, merely shrugged her shoulders and flicked her head to ask if I wanted it. Strange French body language that I had started to figure out. I nodded back. I don't know how much it cost. I don't know how she paid for it on my meagre budget for that trip. I know that it became my most cherished piece of sporting memorabilia.

I wore it a couple of times for gym class in Spioraid Naoimh. I never wore it casually on the street. Too precious to risk. I mostly just took it out to look at it. To savour it. To marvel at its beauty. And sometimes, late in the evening, when there's nobody else around, I carefully unfold it from the shelf where it now sits and still do.

TEN

Flick To Kick

One of my favourite pages in *SHOOT!* was called 'World Wide'. It carried snippets of news from distant countries whose names I often encountered for the first time when reading about some bizarre football-related story. It was there I discovered the Copa Libertadores, exotic clubs like River Plate, Colo Colo and Independiente, and the fact that soccer existed on every corner of the planet.

'Trouble in the African Champions' Cup Final in Conakry, Guinea,' wrote Christopher Davies in a typical entry. 'Home side Hafia beat Mouloudja of Algeria 3–0 in this first leg battle. Two Algerians were sent off for spitting at the referee.'

This was also the place where I first came across the New York Cosmos and the North American Soccer League. The club and the competition were immediately attractive because they were American and, to us, America was then this faraway land of glitz and opportunity that we glimpsed on television. It was Hollywood. It was Jim Rockford. It was *F-Troop*. It was *The Brady Bunch*. Their soccer looked different too. The grass in the photographs was ridiculously green because, in most instances, it was, of course, astro-turf. The stadia were cavernous and spacious and just bloody huge, confirming our childhood impression that everything in the United States was somehow bigger and better.

The Cosmos were an instant fascination because around that time they had Johan Neeskens in their team. Like Cruyff, he was a Dutch icon, so we loved him unconditionally in our house. I was also taken by their white and green shirts – which had a slicker design than the English jerseys we marvelled at each week. I'm not sure why I thought this although it may have had something to do with them wearing numbers on the front as well as the back. Novelty was everything.

Farranlea Park was about as far removed from the Cosmos and Giants Stadium as it was possible to get. Nestling behind an old stone wall on the Farranlea Road, it was a soccer pitch with a serious slope from one sideline to the other and, invariably, a mud patch where the grass used to be down the centre of the field. It was the home of Wilton United FC. The first time I entered this arena I walked in as part of a crack (well, not really) Summerstown United Under-10 team to play a Southside League match.

There were no dressing-rooms (as was the norm back then) so both squads got togged out under the shade of the trees that separated the ground from the GAA field next door. As the Wilton players started to make their way in dribs and drabs onto the field, I immediately noticed a couple of odd things. The person directing these kids, their manager, was a monk. A man in a brown robe with a white rope tied at the waist. An actual monk. A monk like the ones we regularly saw in pairs shuffling around the North Main Street when I went shopping with my mother in town.

That wasn't even the strangest sight. Far more peculiar was the fact they were all wearing full sets of authentic, proper kit. I don't meant they were all wearing roughly the same coloured shirts and shorts like we were. No, this was a matching, real kit. From top to toe. On closer inspection, I discovered that the logo on the front of their shirts was familiar too. It was the unmistakable ball logo of the New York Cosmos. This was too much. I seethed with envy and felt suddenly inferior.

Before the first whistle blew that day, we were beaten. How could we not have been? We looked like Raggyball Rovers, they looked like a serious soccer team, resplendent in gleaming American shirts that made them look faster and stronger. We lost because we were so dazzled by the wonder of their kit that we couldn't possibly concentrate on the task at hand. Or, they might argue, we lost because they were a lot better than us at soccer as well as fashion. They had substance to go with their style.

Inevitably, there was a story about how Wilton United had come across their fantastic gear. According to one of their players who was in my class at school, a character who may or may not have been the most reliable of witnesses, it was all the work of the resourceful and remarkable monk on the sideline. His name was Brother Alfie, and he was a Capuchin based at St Bonaventure's monastery just down the road from the field.

Legend had it that the enterprising Brother Alfie had written to the New York Cosmos asking them to sponsor an impoverished Irish soccer club that was doing Trojan work, keeping boys off the streets and out of crime. Suitably impressed by this plea, boxes of shirts and shorts and socks in all children's sizes were soon winging their way across the Atlantic Ocean.

There were a few problems with this version of events. For starters, Wilton was not an impoverished area, by any means.

And I'm not sure a soccer club owned by Warner Bros would have been that philanthropic either, certainly not to a charity case three thousand miles away in another country. In any case, I wasn't overly concerned with poking holes in the conspiracy theory at the time because I was brimming with jealousy of the boys who got to wear the white and green of Neeskens and the Cosmos every single week!

My neighbour Ian O'Leary started playing for Wilton United around this time. He didn't even like soccer that much and yet suddenly it was like he was almost, by proxy, a member of the New York Cosmos. My envy of him didn't last that long because in the summer of 1982, as we sat in the square in front of our houses, trying to come up with ways of making money, he had an idea. We should go ask Brother Alfie for a job. After all, anyone capable of procuring the most flash sports gear Cork had ever seen could surely figure out a way to help us.

Bold as brass, we cycled the two miles to St Bonaventure's, made our way around the back of a grey, foreboding building and knocked on the door.

'Can we speak to Brother Alfie?' we asked.

The monk who greeted us didn't seem perturbed. Alfie ran a soccer club. Kids probably came calling all the time.

'We're looking for summer jobs,' said Ian when Alfie appeared. I didn't speak. I stood there suppressing my urge to ask him straight out about his long-distance relationship with the fabled Cosmos.

Think about this tableau: Ian was twelve; I was eleven, and here we were asking a monk that one of us kind of knew through soccer for gainful employment. Amazingly, Brother Alfie wasn't the slightest bit fazed by the request.

'Come back tomorrow around 9am and wear dirty clothes.'

So we did. He told us where to put our bikes then handed us paint brushes and set us to work whitewashing walls in a long corridor. I'm not sure whether those walls even needed to be painted or whether he was just being charitable: either way we set about the task with gusto. Like real painters, we even brought a radio with us on the second day to listen to music as we rolled Valspar emulsion from floor to ceiling. Every now and again a monk shuttled past and complimented our handiwork.

Each lunchtime, Alfie appeared and escorted us down to the kitchen where we were handed tureens of thick, steaming soup and small mountains of coarsely-cut homemade brown bread. I didn't eat brown bread but wolfed it down anyway because I didn't want to offend our hosts and risk losing our contract. Not that there was a contract or anything. We never knew how much we were going to be paid and daren't ask. Our parents had no problems with the arrangement, thinking, as per people of their generation, if we were spending our days in a monastery, we couldn't come to much harm.

As the days went on we got more comfortable in the surroundings and started to explore the building. In a room off one hallway, we discovered a kitchenette with a SodaStream. There were two types of kids in our lives: those who had SodaStreams and those who were insanely jealous of them. Within minutes, we had mastered the intricacies of the machine and thereafter we worked like demented dervishes, high on sugar after quaffing bottles and bottles of carbonated drinks. We were no longer so much painting the walls as bouncing off them.

The willful, greedy, and unauthorised use of the SodaStream may or may not have been why, at the end of our second week, Brother Alfie sent us on our way. He assured us that the Capuchin friars were very pleased with the work we did but that we should go off and enjoy our summer holidays. Like kids. Sound advice. Except for one thing. We'd earned £15 each for the fortnight's work and that wasn't anywhere near the target of £100 that I'd set myself – that being the price of the bike of my dreams. I still needed money then. Badly.

The late 1970s and early '80s were a golden age for cool bicycles. Raleigh had come out with three magnificent creations – even their names reeked of excitement – the Chopper, the Grifter and the Burner. Each had very different merits. The Chopper had the raised handlebars and distinctive high-backed seat of an Easy Rider motorbike with a gear stick in the centre of the frame like in a car. The Grifter was more dynamic and sporty yet equally unique, boasting gears on the handlebars and the type of thick tyres that encouraged kids to go leaping off kerbs; a jump of all of six inches. The Burner was built for wheelies and tricks, and came in chrome and dayglo colour schemes with thick spokes in the wheels that were almost futuristic.

These were the bikes every young boy dreamed of owning; these were the bikes I dreamed of owning. My parents though had other ideas. They had a perfectly good bike in mind for me. It was a Triumph 20. I'm not sure what shade of green the manufacturers called the paint job on it, but I like to think it was listed on the palette as 'disgusting green'. Having been (barely) used by my two older sisters (a warning sign of its inherent lack of cool), this contraption, replete with flower stickers on the main frame (Anne's handiwork!), now fell to me. The least grateful recipient ever.

Kids on Choppers, Grifters and Burners could bust moves and throw shapes. They could pull wheelies while going down the street at high speed. They could make dramatic entrances into our square, skidding on the gravel and turning at the same time, sometimes even kicking up wisps of dust clouds. I could do none of these things. I came sauntering along on my Triumph 20 with a wicker basket on the front looking like I was on my leisurely way to a picnic in Devon with The Famous Five.

'Can't we get me a proper bike?' I asked. Repeatedly.

'This is a proper bike,' said my mother, abruptly and repeatedly.

'A boy's bike!'

'This'll do you grand.'

There was no point bringing my father into the argument. My mother held the purse strings. Tightly. And when she reeled out the phrase 'this'll do you grand' I knew I was doomed. That was her stock response to every complaint I made about being at the bottom of the family food chain, the perfect location for receiving hand-me-downs.

'Can I get new sneakers?'

'Tommy's old ones will do you grand.'

'They're manky.'

'They'll be grand after I wash them and get you new laces.'

Grand. A strange word to grow up hating but she left me no choice.

Sometimes, if he was elsewhere, I borrowed Tommy's five-speed Raleigh Scorpio, a burnt-orange racing bike that he'd bought with his confirmation money. It was too big for me. I could barely get my leg over the crossbar and stopping in a hurry was so perilous that more than once I suffered injuries of a type that endangered my future chances of having a family. It was worth the pain because at least on board that ride I could go fast and keep up with my friends. The biggest issue, of course, was the risk Tommy would come back in need of the bike, find it missing from the shed and proceed to kill me.

My parents didn't understand that it was especially crucial to have a proper bicycle at this time because we spent most of our days trying to imitate and emulate Frank Poncherello, the coolest motorbike cop in the entire California Highway Patrol. *CHiPs* was can't-miss television every Saturday night. Once we heard the opening riff of the theme tune: 'Dan Dan Denan Dan…', we were transported for the next hour from the dank and damp of Cork to the sunnier climes of southern California. Dan dun de ne daaaaan.

Unlike my parents' grittier favourite *The Streets of San Francisco*, the sun always shone on *CHiPs*. If it didn't, Ponch, as he was known to his friends and us, brightened up every scene with his effervescent teeth. There were breathtaking car chases, almost always precipitated by Ponch and his partner, Jon Baker, having to slow down first to do a u-turn in the middle of the highway and soundtracked by jazz funk instrumentals. Bad guys got their comeuppance a couple of minutes before the end of each episode, the timely denouement allowing just enough space for Ponch to head off on a date with a beautiful woman he met while solving the latest crime.

All of that was just background noise to us. We were intoxicated by Ponch and Jon cruising the impossibly wide highways and byways on their motorbikes then speeding up when they went in hot pursuit of villains. We wanted to cruise around just like them – even if our streets were narrower and nearly always wet with rain. Emulating crime-fighting motorbike cops was difficult, nay impossible, perched atop a Triumph 20, a bicycle more suited for dawdling along country lanes than chasing down speeding bandits in a Ford Thunderbird on the open road. Still, I tried my best.

I might not have been able to buy a new bike with the money earned from the Capuchins that summer but I splurged on a pair of walkie-talkies that I saw in Kilgrew's on North Main Street. As was invariably the way with walkie-talkies, they never quite worked no matter how new the batteries we put in were or how many times we said 'Roger!' and '10–4' while pressing the talk button. Undeterred, I kept them attached to the bike anyway. Anything to try to make it look cooler. An impossible task.

My quest to fund the purchase of a Grifter, my preferred choice in the range available, had brought me to St Bonaventure's to dabble in painting. It also caused me to sign on as a newspaper delivery boy for Dawson's, a shop in Ballyphehane, around the corner from my grandparents.

'See, I told you that basket would come in useful,' said my father when I told him that I had returned to gainful employment.

The basket was indeed useful but the bike remained a constant embarrassment. As we gathered outside the shop in the early morning waiting for our batches of papers to be handed to us, the other delivery boys were sitting astride racers, Choppers and Grifters. I was straddling the Triumph 20, trying and miserably failing to appear cool and nonchalant. Every time somebody laughed I just presumed they were sniggering at my not so trusty steed. Although, that may have just been in my head.

I lasted a couple of weeks at that gig too. I blew the first wage at Baldy's sweet shop on the way home. The second I splurged on a Panini sticker album for the forthcoming soccer season. A new bike would have to wait until my confirmation the following year. That was the way of it for most kids in that time.

Traditionally some combination of their confirmation money and their parents' largesse was used to finance a new bike in time for secondary school because that would be their mode of transport to get there.

In the early summer of 1983 then I finally retired the Triumph 20 to the shed where I watched it happily rust for years after. In its stead, I took possession of a gold, 10-speed Viking racer. I'd grown out of Choppers and Grifters at that point, and, Tom assured me, I needed a serious bike with proper gears to make the three-mile round trip to Coláiste an Spioraid Naoimh in Bishopstown five days a week. Speed was essential when navigating the Wilton roundabout, a traffic flow device that appeared to operate on the principle 'who dares wins, and who loses ends up jousting with an 18-wheeler articulated lorry and being transported to the conveniently located Regional Hospital on the far side of the road'.

On wet days, our mothers made us put on oilskins more suited to fishermen trawling for crabs in the Bering Sea. We sweated our way up the Alpe d'Huez of Wilton Avenue, the last nose-bleeding incline before school. This meant we arrived soaked on the inside and out, and then sat in classrooms going from sopping wet to merely damp by the end of the day. If your bike was out of action, a friend gave you a crosser or allowed you to sit on his backer and never complained about dragging the extra weight. If you had training, you carried a gear bag on your back and balanced a hurley on the handlebars. These were quite the work-outs.

The Viking opened up the wider world to me. Now, I could cycle as far as I wanted as long as I was back for my tea. Now, I could cycle into town. I wasn't yet cool enough to want to walk around the city centre in a pair of black suede brothel-creepers with a Golden Discs bag in my hand showcasing my latest record purchase. That came later. Still stuck somewhere between boy and man-child, I just wanted to cycle to a little shop off the South Mall called Planes, Boats and Trains.

This was a time when Cork boys could be divided into different camps according to their reading habits. In one corner, there were those of a militaristic bent who read *Warlord, Hotspur* and *Commando* comics religiously. They peppered their conversations with foreign phrases like 'Gott im Himmel' and 'Sacre Bleu' that they'd picked up in these stories of derring-do. The most devout of their number mailed off postal orders and application forms to join the *Warlord* secret agent club, an ID they subsequently kept in a specially issued wallet. Conveniently located just in case anybody wanted to look in the wallet to find out if they really were secret agents.

In the other corner stood those of us consumed by *SHOOT!*, *Roy of the Rovers* and *Tiger*. Sure, there was some crossover between the two demographics but not that much. Like the rockers and the mods in Brighton, albeit without the outbreaks of violence, the two factions spent a lot of time hanging around the same place. That was Planes, Boats and Trains on Princes Street. As toys store go, it was like something from a Hollywood movie, a cornucopia of sights and sounds. Model trains and aeroplanes seemed to take up most of the shelf space and were marvellous to look at but held no interest for me.

Those were for the *Warlord* secret agents. They spent much of their spare time painstakingly piecing together intricate Airfix versions of Spitfires, Junkers and Messerschmitt Bf 109s that they bought at Planes, Boats and Trains. The hardcore among them even went to the trouble of hanging the finished aeroplanes from the roofs of their bedrooms by fishing line. I admired their dexterity and their commitment and, possibly, was jealous of their construction ability but I had other fish to fry.

Whenever I had money I made the pilgrimage on my bike to Planes, Boats and Trains to buy paraphernalia for Subbuteo, only the single greatest game ever invented. Certainly, the greatest to ever be invented in Tunbridge Wells. That's where, in the back room of his mother's house, Peter Adolph conceived of a table football game in 1947 that he named after his favourite bird: the *Falco subbuteo*, also known as the Eurasian hobby. The basic kit involved a green baize pitch, two flimsy plastic goals with nets, two teams of 11 miniature players perched on weighted bases, a ball and a vivid imagination. Simple yet magnificent.

'Flick to kick' was the slogan and the object was to usher the ball towards the goal using your thumb and index finger to propel the tiny figurines, or at least propel the semi-circular base they stood on. This was much easier said than done. The keepers were differently-bodied than the outfielders. They had their hands permanently extended upwards in the stretching position and were attached to a stick that went under the goal so the defending player could move them around the area to thwart the attacking team. They looked the part but were essentially powerless against any shot from inside the box that was hit properly.

My first set was the Subbuteo World Cup edition of 1978 with an artist's illustration of Pelé playing for Brazil on the cover. His name wasn't used but it was definitely him. The box contained all the usual stuff but also two floodlight pylons and a gleaming three-inch-tall replica of the Jules Rimet Trophy.

Being an anorak, I knew that this was historically inaccurate – the Rimet had been given permanently to Brazil after the 1970 victory – but it was so shiny and wonderful that I didn't care.

'Thrills galore,' declared the slogan on the cover, 'as you recreate the tremendous excitement of the most famous competition of all – the World Cup! It's all at your fingertips.'

And it was. Always. Well, nearly always.

In an age when parents believed children should be outside whenever possible, staying indoors on a fine day to play Subbuteo wasn't always an option. Staying inside required extenuating circumstances like torrential rain which, of course, was plentiful enough too. On our way upstairs we'd be warned about being too loud. Maybe it was because the houses were all so close together but the parents of Clashduv Road in the 1970s and 1980s were always very concerned about noise pollution and super vigilant when it came to not disturbing the neighbours. Either that or they just didn't want to get headaches from listening to us doing commentaries on matches in our best faux English accents that we'd picked up from listening to the BBC on the radio.

Nearly every game I ever played took place on the floor of the parents' bedroom of whatever house we were in. This was, inevitably, the only room that was big enough to lay out the field and allow space for us to clamber along the sidelines reaching our players. Before a kick could be flicked, there were certain pre-match rituals to be performed. The most crucial of these was the ironing of the baize pitch. Not all mothers were willing to sanction this part of the process, reckoning handing a child a steam iron in a confined space was a potential violation of health and safety regulations. As if.

In that case, we fastidiously smoothed out the inevitable wrinkles, persuading ourselves that we were the Subbuteo equivalent of the groundsman driving a roller across a rutted field to try to make it flat. Then, we contorted our way around the pitch, gymnastically writhing into position, balancing precariously on one hand while trying to dribble and shoot with the other. After a couple of hours of crouching, stretching and careful manoeuvering to avoid breaking any other players under our feet, we rose from the carpet with the tortured gait of the prisoners of war on an episode of *Tenko*.

The sore knees and back ache wouldn't have bothered us half as much if it wasn't for the taunting photographs on the cover of every Subbuteo box showing kids playing the game on tables, while standing fully upright. Now and again I ended up at the house of a school friend and discovered that he played Subbuteo on a table in a spare room or in his garage, and, of course, I was very happy for him. At least I pretended to be while inside I was eaten up with jealousy.

I was entitled to be. They had this extra space attached to their houses, and had tables in there specifically set aside for Subbuteo. The extravagance of it. The pitch was even tacked to the surface. Like on the box or in the photos *SHOOT!* sometimes carried of Subbuteo tournaments. This was how the game was meant to be played. I once trooped home from a house in Summerstown suffused with so much envy about my friend's Subbuteo set-up that I wondered if his family might be interested in adopting me. After all, my reasoning went, I'd spend most of my time in the garage so they'd barely notice I was there in between meals.

It wasn't just the physical toll that playing on your knees took, it was also the attrition rate of players. Despite our best efforts, scarcely a game ended without a player being trod on, the most common injury involving his legs being severed from the base. Surgeons in war zones didn't care as much about saving these limbs as we did. Some people even posited the theory that if you used an excess of super glue on the repair job you might make your player even stronger than he had been originally.

This faulty logic was an obvious byproduct of watching too many episodes of *The Six Million Dollar Man* where the voiceover assured us, 'Gentlemen, we can rebuild him, we have the technology… better, faster, stronger…' Unlike Steve Austin, no matter how much we wished it so, no Subbuteo player ever returned from this type of surgery in an improved state or even restored to their former glory. Bionic they were not.

There were other games that occasionally took our fancy. We had table football, something we later discovered that we should have been calling 'Foosball', a name we never gave it. That was fun too until it developed dead spots on the field where the ball mysteriously came to a stop. We also had Super Striker, which falsely advertised itself as an improvement on Subbuteo because every player had one moveable leg. To shoot the ball you simply had to press down on his head, which had some sort of spring attached to his lower half; clever idea and enjoyable in its way.

But Subbuteo had more to offer. It wasn't just a game. It was a full-time hobby. We bought into the culture surrounding it. There were adverts in *SHOOT!* and *Roy of the Rovers* for new teams and accessories that it was claimed were necessary to 'Add to the big match atmosphere!' Which seemed perfectly reasonable to me, a punter gullible enough to then cycle into town to see if Planes, Boats and Trains had them, and at what price. There might be several reconnaissance missions on the bike before the day came when I had cash in hand and the serial number of the product written out on a piece of paper.

'I'll have an Aston Villa please, I think you'll find they are team number 333.'

These were not mere playthings, they were miniature works of art. I liberated the Villa squad from the green cardboard box like a curator at a museum taking a precious artifact out of storage for cleaning. I wasn't bothered that none of the players had a thick, bushy beard like Dennis Mortimer because there was no greater thrill than placing a new team out on the kitchen table, admiring the numbers 1–11 (as it was and always should be!) carefully etched onto the back of the tiny shirts.

The beauty of Subbuteo was that you could play on your own too. Not just the game but the set-up. Over time, I purchased everything I could afford in my quest for ever greater verisimilitude. I had several policemen, one of them mounted on a horse, just in case any of the fans got a bit rowdy. I placed a photographer crouching behind the goal in the perfect position to take a shot, his camera clung to his face. It took me a while to figure out whether he should be inside or outside the brown picket fences that went around my field, complete with realistic advertising hoardings for Esso and Callard & Bowser Toffee.

I had never been to a match in England but I knew what the ground was supposed to look like. This is why I splurged on absolutely essential extras like a box of six corner flags and a tower for the television cameras, plus the entire crew necessary to broadcast the game. This included a tiny commentator in a sheepskin coat with the very same microphone John Motson used to have clung to his mouth on *Match of the Day*. Subbuteo was nothing if not realistic.

My most extravagant and utterly pointless purchase was a two-tier stand. It was an ugly combination of green and brown, and came with a handful of flat-capped spectators that looked positively lost amid all the empty spaces. Only then did I realise I'd never be able to afford to buy enough boxes of extra supporters to make the stands heave with people like they did on television. Mine looked like a club mired in relegation trouble, struggling to attract fans to its games.

Still, I spent hours happily piecing together the various parts of my Subbuteo ground, then I knelt there marvelling at how much it resembled a real football stadium despite being wedged in the narrow space on the carpet between my parents' bed and the high wardrobe. Confines so tight indeed that merely playing a match there necessitated the removal of the freshly-constructed stand. A lot of trouble to play what the ads assured us and what we well knew to be 'the world's greatest game!'

ELEVEN

All In The Family

On 2 October 1948 an experimental Cork United line-up defeated Shamrock Rovers 3–1 in their first Shield fixture of the new League of Ireland season at The Mardyke. My mother's father, Tommy Morrissey, was in the team that day, that fateful day as it turned out. This was to be United's last appearance at the storied venue they'd bestrode for the previous eight years, during which time they'd garnered five titles, two FAI cups and one double. The following week, the loss-making club was disbanded after a match against Limerick at the Market's Field, the financial woes blamed on the fact that a paltry hundred people in the city had bought season tickets.

My grandfather later handed down what he claimed was his old Cork United jersey to myself and Tom. Predominantly red with a round white collar, the fabric was heavier than what we were used to, and almost hairy to the touch, which made us believe it was at least old. In a terrible laundry accident, our mother shrunk this valuable heirloom in a hot wash but owning that shirt, even in a fun-size version, made us believe every one of his tall tales about the abuse our grandfather used to receive when hugging the left wing down the 'Dyke.

"'I've seen a better pair of wings on a duck!" was what some smart alec shouted,' he told me once, chuckling at the memory of a long-ago afternoon in his athletic prime.

All that remained of the player we glimpsed at the front in sepia-tinted team photographs (when their shirts, tellingly, never, ever had round collars!) was the Brylcreemed hair slicked back off his face. In those fading pictures, he looks every inch a footballer of that age. The shorts are billowy and the shirt tucked in, the boots hobnailed and ankle high, and he has one hand on his right knee, staring down the camera intently.

It was difficult for me to reconcile that almost glamorous, dashing young man with the dishevelled character who sat in an armchair at my grandparents' house on McDonagh Road and asked me to pass him his medicine. At an early age, I realised the 7-UP bottle I handed him was not prescribed by any doctor. It usually contained some sort of alcoholic hooch or whiskey. I knew this because when he wasn't looking I sniffed it and almost threw up from the overpowering whiff.

Despite that, it was always entertaining to be in his orbit because he invariably spun yarns and produced strange sporting objects that he'd picked up on his travels. He once gifted me the most beautiful metal pin with the words Oldham Athletic on it. Carefully clipping it onto my Lord Anthony snorkel jacket, he assured me it was a memento from the time he went on trial at Boundary Park just after the war ended. I loved the trinket and the story. At least until I told my father about it. He examined the badge, shook his head and shattered my illusions, saying something like 'The only trial he's ever been on was in a court.'

Another night, he came through the door rambunctious as ever in his cups, and from somewhere within his Crombie produced a Manchester United away shirt. One of the great Manchester United away shirts, the white one made by Admiral with a v-neck collar and the unmistakable black stripes running down one side of the front. I didn't follow United. But I was smart enough not to tell a well-oiled man that information as he handed it to me like a prize, muttering one of his standard catchphrases, 'For you, señorita, I would kill the bull.'

Another night, he pulled a wooden plaque from under the chair and told me it was mine to keep. Far less exciting than a shirt, it was an excellence award he'd recently received from the Cork Ex-Professional Footballers Association. It had an official-looking FAI stamp on it and, according to the engraving, was given to him 'for exemplary professionalism and an outstanding contribution to soccer'. I brought this bauble home and put it on my shelf next to my street league trophies, which it kind of dwarfed.

My grandfather was also involved in the Ballyphehane boxing club. I'm not sure of his exact role in the set-up but he certainly seemed, or at least acted, important any time we were up there. This may have had something to do with the fact two of his sons, my uncles Paul and Ger, boxed with distinction for the club at that time. They trained at the local community centre on Tory Top Road, up the hill from the Church of the Assumption, across the street from a tiny satellite branch of the Cork City Library.

If my mother had been eager that I should join the library, she was adamant that my brother Tom and I were not allowed to box. Under any circumstances. Ever.

We were allowed to go to fights. That was her only concession. And every December, our grandfather dragged us along to the club's Christmas party and then pressed all manner of fizzy drinks and sweets into our hands. But, regardless of how much we begged and pleaded, we were not permitted to don gloves. Never.

We tried, manfully, to get around this prohibition. From time to time, our grandfather might bring us into the box room of the family home and teach us the rudiments of a good jab and the importance of footwork. Once, he took two pairs of old and battered leather gloves, stuffing leaking through the torn stitches, and gave them to us to take home. We walked to the car with them stuffed under our shirts, out of our mother's sight.

Once we reached the safety of our bedroom back at our own house, we laced them up and threw shapes without ever knowing what we were really doing. That didn't stop us from boxing whenever we had the chance. Invariably, each bout ended when one of us (usually Tom) caught the other (usually me) flush with a full punch that reinforced the savagery of the sport. We regularly lamented the fact that our mother was being so unfair, preventing us from fulfilling our sporting destiny and emulating our uncles. We tried to get our father to mediate but she was not for turning, dismissing all pleas with statements that always included the scary phrase 'brain damage'.

I was too young to comprehend that part of her reasoning for wanting to stop me developing into the next Sugar Ray Leonard. But there was one Sunday morning when I suddenly got a hunch she might be right. It was in a hall somewhere on the north side of Cork. My uncles were fighting and winning. After Paul's bout, I remember being led backstage, as it were, to the dressing-rooms where all the boys togged out and prepped for their contests together. I needed to pee and my grandfather showed me where the toilet was. That was the moment I saw the reality of the fight game. Somebody had Jackson Pollocked blood all over the tiles of the bathroom and the water in the bowl was a deep, disturbing shade of crimson.

I no longer felt the urge to pee. And I no longer felt the urge to box.

A Kerryman called Muiris McGillicuddy was trying to coach a gaggle of awkward Cork teenagers in the art of kicking points from distance. A break in training allowed Eamon Young his chance, and evincing the certitude of somebody who had won an All-Ireland football medal at centre-field — for Cork in 1945 — he made his bold pronouncement.

'A Mhuiris,' he bellowed towards his fellow member of staff at Coláiste an Spioraid Naoimh. 'That's the way we'll beat ye in years to come, that's exactly how we'll do it too, by kicking points long. We won't always be down, you know.'

And, with that, he was gone down the field and out the gap towards Highfield rugby club, his galoshes squelching in the mud, enjoying the quality of his heckle, and so heartened by the prospect of a brighter future for his beloved county that his bald head shook as he went. McGillicuddy smiled too. And well he might; his county had just won their third All-Ireland in a row, their seventh in nine years.

In my childhood, the Cork footballers' annual defeat by Kerry was as much part of summer's ritual as the sun disappearing behind clouds the moment our car reached any beach ever. Over time, it became difficult for my generation not to invest our oppressors with near-mythical powers. Before adulthood bestowed the gift of perspective and allowed us to acknowledge the sheer greatness of Micko Dwyer's team, we could not comprehend exactly why they were so superior. In the absence of logic, our imaginations were especially vulnerable to provocation. My father was no help in this regard.

One winter, he looked up from the *Cork Examiner* he was reading and told me that Eoin Liston might not be coming home from America for the championship. My heart leapt with joy at the thought of Kerry deprived of their giant, talismanic full-forward. Glee soon turned to gloom however as it emerged weeks later that Liston would be back after all. Not only that, according to my father, his face still stuck in the sports pages, he was supposedly keeping fit by training in the Catskill Mountains in upstate New York.

For a child weaned on the televisual adventures of a genial, bearded hillbilly named Grizzly Adams, this was all I needed to hear. Suddenly, I conjured up images of The Bomber trundling up and down the mountain-side, felling trees, frost clinging to his beard, stopping now and again to wrestle fearsome black bears that he subsequently befriended. Not only was he coming back, worse, he was going to come back bigger, better, stronger. When I put this to my father, he just nodded his head in resignation. These were the times we lived in. Hope had turned into the type of four-letter word we learned not to even use.

Of course, Liston mightn't have been doing a whole lot of working-out over there in the States but that didn't quite fit with my childish imaginings of our county neighbours as a different, somehow more dedicated super-race. This was, also, at least in part, my father's fault. He once gave me Mick O'Connell's autobiography, *A Kerry Footballer*. For an impressionable eleven-year-old, there was no way back after that. Again and again, I used to turn to his account of leaving the Sam Maguire behind him in Croke Park after captaining his county to victory in the 1959 All-Ireland.

I'd never even seen proper footage of O'Connell playing but I read the lines '…what was on my mind was the problem of securing my punt above high water mark when I reached the island (Valentia) that night,' and I sighed. I thought all Kerry footballers must be such zealots. He was so dedicated that he didn't even bother to stay to celebrate winning the championship. What chance did we possibly have against men for whom the actual trophy was only an afterthought? And why, oh why, did my father feed my insecurities by giving the book in the first place?

Around about the same time, he gave me Tim Horgan's *Cork's Hurling Story*, and Val Dorgan's biography of Christy Ring. I hardly needed to read those two wonderful tomes to reinforce my superiority complex about Cork hurling. After all between the ages of five and fifteen, I saw the county win five All-Irelands. We savoured those wins together but it was in our devotion to the long-suffering footballers that father and son forged a peculiar bond. Supporting the hurlers was easy and mostly fun, following the footballers was a grim pilgrimage with no guarantee of any respite at the end.

Yet, there was something noble and warrior-like about Kevin Kehily, Christy Ryan and the rest trotting out there every summer to try to put a halt to the juggernaut of Micko Dwyer and the greatest team the game had ever seen.

At my father's urging, I once attended a senior county football trial in the driving rain over at the Barrs' club. Like a scout prospecting for talent, I watched closely, hoping to bring home news of some wunderkind that was about to change our fortunes. I couldn't find any but I did walk onto the field at the end to ask some rather bemused trialists for their autographs as they trudged off the muddy pitch. They were as unimpressed by my *Scoop!* autograph book as Johnny Giles had been.

Perhaps the worst of it was I had no memory of things ever being any different. My father unfurled stories of the 1973 Cork team so often that I knew them by heart. I listened even though I'd heard them all before, wondered if I would ever know such a powerful bunch of men in the red jersey, and cursed the era I was born. My father's was a generation that wrapped endless anecdotes about Declan Barron's fielding and Jimmy Barry-Murphy's crewcut around themselves like comfort blankets even as their kids were shivering through the nuclear winter of the Kerry hegemony.

'Barron retired from inter-county too early,' he lamented during every post-mortem. 'Those dirty feckers in green and gold blackguarded Jimmy out of the football.'

In such ghastly circumstances, I sought warmth in the strangest of places. When Pat Spillane reached the world final of television's *Superstars*, my initial jealousy at the sight of a Kerryman on the world stage turned to glee. As he took his place among bronzed and toned athletes from all over the planet, his vaguely obscene shorts revealed what were unquestionably the whitest legs in international sport. We laughed for days at the spectacle. In the absence of any chance of actually beating Kerry, we had to find little triumphs where we could.

A character by the name of Sweeney wrote an *Evening Echo* column with just that purpose, leavening our depression with his wit. On Saturday evenings in the summer, my father used to read his work aloud to me and there was solace to be gleaned from his relentless lampooning of the Kerry manager's annual post-Munster final condescension about Cork always giving his side their most difficult game in the championship. His finest article culminated in Micko, unable to finish his speech due to the onset of maniacal laughter, being carried away, howling, by men in white coats.

I might have been a kid, but I was already old enough to appreciate that no journalist ever captured the angst of his audience better than Sweeney.

And then the most amazing thing happened. The morning of 17 July 1983 dawned wet and gloomy, rain pelting down, the wind howling. A classic summer's day. My father surveyed the scene through the living-room window and he started to waver about whether or not to make the trek to Páirc Uí Chaoimh for the Munster football final that day. We never once made the trek to see Cork versus Kerry in Killarney because, as he so lyrically put it, 'I wouldn't give those bastards my money!' But we never missed a game in the Park. Until then.

I could see he was humming and hawing as the morning wore on and the rain didn't let up. Finally, he decided that the inclement weather, the prospect of one more hiding and the inevitable torture of listening to the Kerry faithful in the pubs afterwards was too much to take.

'I think we'll leave it for today, boy,' he said.

I didn't even complain. I, too, was already heartily sick of the beat-downs. So we sat at home, not five miles from Páirc Uí Chaoimh, listening to the radio as Tadhg Murphy plundered a last-minute goal for a Cork victory and his place in folklore. I should have been angry at missing out on history. But I couldn't be because I was too delirious at the result. We gorged ourselves on the highlights on *The Sunday Game* that night. Watching the action unfold in the certain knowledge that Cork would fashion a victory right at the death was a whole different type of thrill of the most delicious kind.

By the next summer, of course, normal service had been resumed. Kerry were back on top and my father saw their dastardly influence everywhere he looked.

'How did you get on today?' he asked after I came in the door from a match with Spioraid Naoimh.

'I was a sub,' I said. 'Only got on for the last fifteen minutes.'

'Who's running the team?'

'McGillicuddy.'

'The Kerry fella?

'Yeah.'

'Sure, he probably has it in for you because you're from Cork.'

There might have been logic in there somewhere except for the fact the fifteen players who started ahead of me were all from Cork too. Still, that's how paranoid we were about the green and gold. I say we because, of course, nobody influences your sporting education quite like your father. Mine visited upon me all of his prejudices and his passions. For better and for worse.

On Wednesday evenings in winter, he joined Tommy and me to play darts in our tiny bedroom, the battered radio liberated from the kitchen, tuned into the crackling signal of European Cup soccer matches being broadcast on BBC. Between trips to the oche, he sat on the bottom bunk and regaled us with the recurring tale of how his own promising arrows career had been stymied by an afternoon spent road bowling before a crucial fixture. Apparently, a few hours throwing the heavy iron ball along the winding back roads out by Cork airport wasn't conducive to a man retaining his crucial feel for lightweight tungsten.

In summer, he hurled with us on the hard, wet sand of every beach we ever visited, beseeching his kids in vain to try to hit off our weaker sides, and always refusing my blasphemous request to substitute a tennis ball for the sliotar.

'When they start playing with tennis balls, we'll start using them,' he said.

I found that regulation as annoying as his insistence that I practice hitting off the left. Nothing is less fun than throwing a sliotar in the air on a windswept strand and airballing it time after time. Although there was no evidence he'd ever meaningfully held a hurley himself, a lack of experience never diminished his enthusiasm for any game and didn't stop him serving as a hurling and football selector on several under-age county championship-winning teams when Tom played for Bishopstown.

According to all available records, my father had never swung an actual golf club in anger or even set foot inside one either but, during the brief, annual spell around the British Open when we'd embrace that sport, he'd help me mow a miniature putting green in the back garden, with an empty Batchelors Peas tin serving as the cup for the hole. Then he'd leave me to practice before we'd go to head to head.

From dewy Sunday mornings before street league matches trying to teach an awkward child to put his toe under the ball before picking it off the ground to lazy afternoons watching English county cricket when multi-channel finally came to our house, my father's interests were wide-ranging. Whether he played before or what he played with us mattered not a jot because he exhibited a love of every sport and evangelised about nearly all of them. Except rugby.

The comfort of the armchair from where he sat sentry on the sporting universe never diminished his capacity for joining in with his kids though. His participation in our every sporting misadventure was never measured by the clock because he always seemed to have time to give. He was never too busy to attempt to coach or, at least, never resilient enough to resist my constant imploring for him to come outside. Just in passing, in those cameos, he communicated an enduring love of all things Cork which was, of course, our birthright.

Like so many men and boys, so many fathers and sons, in Irish households then, there was a lot unspoken between us, so much unsaid so often, except when it came to teams and heroes and villains and matches won and lost. There were no uncomfortable silences then. No awkward gaps in the narrative. No lack of raw emotion. In that much, always and forever more, the sporting world was our enduring bond.

I was standing in the kitchen, waiting for my mother to turn around. I wanted to see her face when she answered me.

'You're coming to the match right?' I asked.

'I am,' she said, sounding ever so slightly exasperated by the question.

'You said you'd come if we got to the final and this is the final.'

'I know that.' Getting a little irritated now, the voice rising a tad. 'I'll be there.'

'You're not lying now?' The classic child's interrogation technique of asking questions until the subject breaks.

'Will you stop? We're going to follow you out.'

'You're not just saying that to shut me up now.'

'You're going to be late. Get out that door and good luck.'

An hour later, halfway through the Bishopstown Under-10 football street league final in 1981, I still hadn't had a meaningful touch. This was partly due to being stuck in corner-forward on one of those days when the ball hardly came into our section of the field. But there was something else distracting me too. Where was my mother? She said she was coming. She promised. But there were a lot of parents there, more than I'd ever seen at a game before, and I couldn't find her. So I kept looking. All around.

The few times the ball did come near where I was stationed, my man reacted first because he was paying attention. I wasn't. I had one eye on the action, but I was preoccupied. I was scanning through the wire fence to see if she was really there. I mean, she promised. She had to be. She didn't lie, did she?

Eventually, I found her. She was there all right. With my nan too. They were difficult to find because, unlike some of the other parents, my mother wasn't inclined to shout or do anything untoward like that. She was a silent and possibly bemused observer. But she was there, and that was all that mattered. Finally, I could play in peace. Finally, I could play. And right at the finish, I ended up scoring the winning goal after blatantly pushing an overgrown full-back named Pat Cuthbert out of the way first.

I once tried to figure out how many matches my mother saw me play as a child. I know it was fewer than ten. It may even have been fewer than five. It was a struggle to remember any other appearances by her on the sidelines with great clarity. As it would be for anybody of my or older generations. In terms of parental involvement, those were different times. A lot of parents didn't attend the games their kids played. Most who did were fathers and they were usually involved in some capacity in running the team or helping out.

My father brought me to nearly every game I ever played. My mother was scarcely present in those fields at all. That was the way of it. Nobody thought it odd. Nobody complained. It only seems strange now that we live in a more involved era, where parents are present for every training session and scrimmage.

That's not to say our mothers were not supportive of our putative careers. Oh, they were. My mother attended very few of my matches yet she was a huge presence at all of them. In her own ways, she contributed just as much. If not more.

I don't think I ever once opened a gear bag in a dressing-room, be it hurling, Gaelic football or soccer, that didn't have everything I needed perfectly packed inside. I don't mean that the required socks and shorts and shirt were tucked in there. I mean every item of clothing had not only been washed but dried, sometimes by the coal fire, then ironed and folded and made ready with what was obviously so much great care. Not by me. For me. By my mother.

Team-mates on either side of me might unfurl jerseys that reeked of previous battles, unleashing sweat clouds of toxic ammonia into the already putrid air. Meanwhile, oftentimes, my biggest struggle was tearing open the separate Dunnes Stores plastic bags into which she had so lovingly folded every item of clothing that I needed. Right down to the Mikasa gloves with the black pimples on them if it was a Gaelic football match.

Her selfless devotion ensured I never took the field appearing anything less than pristine and always smelling impossibly fresh. If the shorts were white, she'd have added bleach to the wash. If there were particularly stubborn mud stains on them, she regarded those as a personal challenge to her standards of hygiene. No son of hers was going into the fray without resembling one of the full-colour pre-season photographs of footballers in gleaming, new kit, the ones that we ogled every August in the pages of *SHOOT!*.

Indeed, if looking the part had been any measure of true athletic ability, I would have scored points for Cork in both codes and played on the left side of midfield for Ireland at the 1994 World Cup. I never played quite as well as I togged out. That would have been an impossible standard to reach.

My mother was centrally involved in the pre-match routine too. On weekend mornings, she stood by the stove preparing massive pots of Flahavan's Progress Oatlets; thick and creamy porridge, sprinkled with sugar, or if the funds were good, maybe even a couple of spoons of honey. It was so irresistible that I could never wait for it to cool so I gulped down great mouthfuls that left my tongue lightly blistered. But in the best way.

Whatever other reason I inevitably later found to blame my failure to fulfill my sporting dream that particular day, it was never dietary. She ensured I never left the house unless I was fully loaded and ready to go. A smile on her face in the hallway as she went through the checklist to make sure nothing was forgotten then, the worst part, she'd lick her fingers and smooth over the fringe of my hair as I recoiled.

'Mam! Mam! Please stop!'

In the admittedly unreliable highlight reel of my memory, we were constantly playing matches in driving rain. Each one of those savage Saturday mornings culminated in me returning to find her standing in the hallway, ushering me to a toasty kitchen where a steaming bowl of oxtail soup and ramparts of buttered white Cuthbert's bread were waiting to, as she described it, 'get a bit of heat back into you'.

If the timing of a game meant I missed Sunday dinner with the family, she put aside an overburdened plate for me. This was heated up and handed to me, to be eaten on my lap in front of the telly and in front of a coal fire blazing. A flagrant relaxation of the usual dining rules. A special treat. It says much about the quality of my athletic exploits that some of my fondest memories of the mid-'80s revolve around watching matches on the television while belatedly wolfing down a roast and wondering whether mam had kept some trifle for me too. She did. Of course she did.

Once my food had been served, she disappeared from sight. It was only years later I realised that was the time she was going through the gear bag, separating the whites from the rest, placing the boots on the back step (a bridge too far even for her) and starting the clean-up of the shirts and shorts even though the next game might be a week away. Time was of the essence because, like every Irish mother, she spent a large part of her existence in the pre-electric dryer era worried about rain.

'There's not a bit of drying there,' she said, looking out the rain-soaked kitchen window as if trying to stare down the weather gods.

My mother was part of a resourceful generation of working-class women who grew up with so little that they were magnificent at making something out of nothing. She was into upcycling clothes and gear decades before it became fashionable. No matter how little was going spare, money could be found somewhere for anything sports-related. And, if funds were low, she improvised.

For instance, the white Steve Heighways that were my first ever pair of boots (see chapter nine), she convinced me they came with an illustrious pedigree. She told me an impressive backstory about how they had been worn by my uncles with distinction before being handed on to Tom and then down to me, the inheritor of a noble tradition. I later discovered this was a yarn spun out of pure cloth. Having actually bought them second-hand from one of the clothes stalls she loved to browse along the Coal Quay on Saturday mornings, she reckoned an alternative origin myth might send me onto the field with more of a pep in my step. And, of course, she was right.

For somebody who didn't go to games, she did have very strict ideas about sport though. Boxing wasn't the only pastime she vigorously opposed. Darts was a pub game that would take children down the wrong path even if they were playing at home. It took some persuasion before we were even allowed to get a board for the bedroom. Snooker was also dismissed, the pastime of corner boys. Trying to get her to give me money to pay for an hour's light at The Mardyke Club had a blood from stone vibe about it. She'd have sooner given cash for cigarettes than for potting blacks.

'That's only for bowsies.'

My mother was not unique. She was, like tens of thousands of other remarkable Irish mothers of that time, simply doing what she perceived to be her job. Much of her work was unseen and too often we under-appreciated just how magnificent she was at it: raising kids, fostering their dreams and filling their bellies. Our fathers may have basked in whatever slivers of reflected glory were available on the sidelines when things went well. It was our unsung mothers who underpinned the whole operation by keeping the home fires burning regardless of the results.

For my mam, there was absolutely no sulking in defeat and, even more vehemently, no boasting in victory: win with class; lose with class. That was her dictum. And, always, no matter whether you were gleeful or glum, there was a simple interrogation to remind you of what sport was supposed to be about.

'Did you try your best and did you enjoy it?' she asked every time.

'I did,' I replied, knowing that's what she wanted to hear. 'And that's all that matters really.'

If I close my eyes, I can see her standing in the hallway of a house in Togher saying those words. Still.

TWELVE

Seeing Stars

We were almost finished getting our school uniforms back on when one of the men in charge started to usher us all into the low-ceilinged dressing-room next door. There, another man with a thick, salt and pepper beard stood up on the bench along one wall with a sheet of paper in his hands. The instructions were simple enough. If he called your name, you had made the team. If he didn't call your name, you could leave. Maybe 30 seconds had passed when I heard 'David Hannigan, Glasheen'. I didn't react. At least not outwardly. Inwardly, my stomach lurched like a ball about to bounce off the floor beneath my feet.

This was the final trial for the Cork Sciath Na Scol Under-12 Gaelic football team. And I had made the cut. I wasn't surprised. I had just enjoyed one of those special games we all fantasised about. Everywhere I went, the ball seemed to magically appear. Every time I competed for it, it somehow ended up in my grasp. On four occasions, I took possession near enough to the goalposts to shoot and curled each one over with my left, the kind of perfect kicks I knew were going to be points the moment they left my boot.

Halfway through the second half I was substituted and I knew then, the way you always know in these circumstances, that I had done enough. I was going to be picked.

Outside the dressing-rooms, Tom was standing in among the small gaggles of parents and teachers. About to turn fifteen, he had been awarded a half-day to accompany me to the trial. My mother was notoriously liberal in her dispensation of half-days. She was also desperate not to have to go with me herself.

I didn't have to tell Tom the news. He could see it in my smile and he congratulated me by punching me on the shoulder. The punch of a proud brother delivered with real emotion.

'Come on, we better go ring Dad!' he said, fishing in his jeans pocket for the coins my mother had pressed into his hand before we left. My father had just started working as a porter in Allied Irish Bank on Patrick Street and hadn't been there long enough to wangle a half-day to go to see his child play a match, even as big a game as a trial for the Cork Under-12 Gaelic football team!

So we sprinted the short distance from the Barrs' club to Togher post office on the corner with Tramore Road. The phone was on the wall just inside the door, one of those complicated contraptions with two buttons that said A and B. Tommy had the phone number on a piece of paper in his pocket. He got through to my father but instantly handed me the receiver. He didn't want to steal my thunder.

'I made the team!' I shouted loud enough for the whole post office to hear.

'Brilliant boy!' he replied.

'I scored four points and I gave some great passes and…'

Words spilled out of me in an excited torrent. This was it. I was going to play for Cork. My serious sporting life started here. Eventually, Tom spared my father any more of my rambling about my impending greatness and wrestled the phone back.

Two weeks later, I was given a day off school to go and play for Cork. I got the number 10 bus into town with my father and he walked me to the Opera House where the Sciath na Scol squads (hurlers and handballers travelled too) were meeting before travelling to Semple Stadium to take on Tipperary.

Getting on a Cork team bus outside the Cork Opera House. This was the big time. Boys from all corners of the city clambering aboard, trying not to make eye contact with rivals from clubs they hated. Vague nods of recognition towards those they might have crossed swords with during the year and who they remembered with more fondness. Gear bags into the overhead locker above the seat. This was the real thing all right. Cork going to Thurles to play Tipp. What sport was all about.

Before the game, the buses pulled into a monastery or school, a grey building where they sat us at long rectangular tables and fed us soup. Well, some of us. There were peas in the soup. I didn't eat peas. I didn't eat the soup. I just loaded up on the bread that came with it. A rookie mistake. I was starving for the rest of the day.

A couple of hours later, I ran out onto the fabled sward of Semple Stadium as the rain bucketed down. It was a thrill. A soggier thrill than I hoped for but a thrill nonetheless. I took my spot at the top of the left, shook hands with my man, and after that I didn't touch the ball, spending most of the time listening to my tummy rumble. I made a valiant attempt to gather one ball that came down the line but it squirmed out of play ahead of my spectacular slide. I almost blocked down their full-back at one point but he followed through on my fingers and made them sting.

At half-time I was called ashore. Justifiably. I watched the rest of the game from the bench, water dripping down the back of my neck. Aside from the moments when I marvelled at the play of a fair-haired future Cork star named Colin Corkery, I wished the whole thing to be over. The game ended in a draw and then something happened that was far worse than my failure to perform. They took back the jerseys!

I couldn't believe it. I had convinced myself beforehand that, whatever else transpired, we would be allowed to keep the red shirts as mementoes of the day. As the bearded man from the original trial walked around collecting them, I did, just for a second, consider trying to steal mine. If ever theft was justified, this was it. Then, I figured this kind of larceny might get me in trouble at school so I thought better of it.

A couple of weeks later, Mr McCarthy came into our classroom and went into a huddle with Mr Nelligan up by the board. He then asked me to stand up and started to make a speech. My stomach felt suddenly queasy. I was worried he'd mention me being taken off at half-time but he was far too kind for that. Instead, he congratulated me on my selection for the Cork team and spoke of what an honour it was to represent my county in Semple Stadium, of all places. He assured me that if I kept going I would no doubt wear the red jersey again.

I believed him too because Mr McCarthy coached the school football teams so he obviously knew his stuff. Indeed, my faith in his judgement was such that as I walked up to the top of the room so he could hand me the medal every player received for playing, the spring returned to my step. By the time I sat down, my confidence was such that I spent a large part of the rest of the day pondering a serious conundrum. How could I possibly balance playing for Cork with the needs of my career manning the left side of midfield for Aston Villa and Ireland? I knew Kevin Moran had briefly juggled Manchester United and the Dubs and I wondered if everybody involved would be as accommodating of me when the time came.

'Do you think Aston Villa will allow me play for Cork every summer?' I asked my father as I showed him the medal that night.

'I'm sure they will. They'll probably be glad of you keeping fit.'

Frank O'Sullivan was the genial manager of the Summerstown United Under-14s. An electrician by trade, he used his work van as our team bus. For away matches, a couple of us sat in the front while as many as could reasonably fit were stashed in the back, perched precariously in between shelves of fuses, plugs, wires and the other tools of his profession. Every bump in the road was an adventure but the conditions of the journey didn't matter because Frankie Sull, as we affectionately called him, was the most generous, funny and warm character. We loved, especially, his live commentary during every match.

'Fair play to you, Davey boy, me swan in the lough,' he shouted whenever I scored a goal. The way he bellowed the most curious turns of phrase – 'Dowtcha me daza, me flower!' – made us laugh and inspired us to greater heights. Who wouldn't want to do something on the pitch to elicit that response from the man on the sideline? Every time we took the field, we were all looking to impress him, just to find out if he had any other curious colloquialisms in his arsenal that we hadn't heard before.

There was only one morning I remember Frankie Sull being rendered more or less speechless. We had travelled to

Whitechurch on the outskirts of the city to play a cup match against Rockmount, a team a division above us. A team we knew only by reputation. And that Saturday we discovered very quickly why they had a reputation. Every side we played had a couple of star players; Rockmount had some of the best the city had ever seen.

Alan O'Sullivan had blond hair and the type of floppy fringe that wouldn't have been out of place on a member of ABC. He wasn't bigger than us. He didn't appear stronger. He just looked normal as he took his place wide on the left. From the kick-off, Rockmount tipped and tapped it around then pushed the ball out to him. He collected it just inside his own half, very far from danger, and then he set off down the wing.

He dropped a shoulder and went past one of us. Then he did some sort of a thing with his feet to ghost past another. He wasn't moving at great speed. He had that languid pace of somebody in complete control of the ball and their body, travelling just as fast as the task required him to. No faster until the occasion demanded a higher gear.

Our centre-halves, big, burly boys capable of inflicting pain if needs be, converged upon him. One stuck out a malicious leg a millisecond after he'd already passed by. The other saw this so he went to grab him with both hands and ended up with his fingers flailing in vain at the fabric of the jersey. O'Sullivan was moving along the edge of the box now, another defender hovering into view about to try and, inevitably, fail to check his progress.

Having done all this with the ball apparently glued to his left, he pulled back his right to shoot with venom. The ball cannoned off the crossbar with an impressive thud and then flew over as our goalkeeper watched on helpless. Stricken. Impressed.

I witnessed hundreds, maybe thousands of goals scored in the games that I played. But I remember that near miss with greater clarity than any of them. The whole movement was so balletic and beautiful. There was a certain grace about the way he rode tackles, evaded attempted assaults, and turned defenders inside out. Years later, I read Paddy Crerand's famous quote about George Best giving opponents a case of 'twisted blood' and I understood exactly what he meant because that was what I'd seen Alan O'Sullivan do.

From my vantage point in the middle of midfield on that day, the sight of this boy in full flow was mesmeric enough to stop me even bothering to track back. I was too hypnotised by the natural beauty and the poetry of the movement to remember I had a job to do for my team.

For all the stories we heard about this team having a couple of special players, nothing prepared us for the full-on experience. Most sides in our age groups had a couple of stars, a lot of average kids, and a couple of passengers. Rockmount didn't do average or passengers.

At the back, Paul McCarthy was a centre-half to whom the ball appeared magnetically attracted. Once it went anywhere near the box, he met it with his head or his foot. For corners, he sidled up field with menace before hurling himself at anything flying through the air. Broad-chested, tall and athletic, against us that morning, he played like a man who never had to bother getting out of second gear, somebody saving himself for more serious engagements. He was destined to captain the Irish Under-21s and to start over five hundred first team games in England with Brighton, Wycombe Wanderers and Oxford United.

In midfield, there was a diminutive dynamo with a mullet who seemed to hoover up every loose ball before passing unerringly to a team-mate. Hard in the tackle for a fella his size, he was complaining to his colleagues the whole time even as they lorded it over us with ease. A relentless, narky force of nature, he covered an immense amount of ground; one moment he was threatening in our six-yard box, the next he was tracking back on the edge of his own area. That morning I gave up trying to compete with him very quickly. I knew I was out of my depth. His name was Roy Keane.

Yet the future Manchester United and Ireland captain did not leave an impression quite like Alan O'Sullivan in his magnificent pomp. This character was an up close glimpse of something otherworldly. One of those cameos that made me begin to realise that no matter how hard I trained or dedicated myself, I was never ever going to rise to the top of this sport. No amount of juggling the ball in my spare time would empower me with his preternatural gifts. No physical fitness regime to make myself stronger could possibly bridge the yawning gap between my effort and his effortlessness. Here was empirical proof of that.

Of course, I looked at his boots when I got up next to him. I needed to check if there was something different about them, something affording him special powers. There is something about the boy child that we think there has to be an extraneous factor giving a peer an edge over us. It can't be anything innate like ability. But that's what it was because he was wearing regular Adidas boots. Nothing special about them at all. Except his feet in them.

The rest of that match is a blur of those green and gold Rockmount jerseys weaving their way through us and scoring at will. Most of them were a year younger than us, dominating an age group above them, and playing a game with which we were not familiar. By the second half, we were time-wasting to try to keep the score down – like rugby players we kicked for touch with length and purpose. Finally, thankfully, in the traditional way of merciful Cork Schoolboys' League referees, the fight was stopped before we bled all the way into double figures.

'That Sullivan boy kind of reminds me of Matthews,' said Frankie Sull in the van on the way home.

'Who's Matthews?' we asked.

'Stanley Matthews. Ask your fathers about him.'

Later that season, I got another look at the Rockmount players from a different angle. Every club in Cork was invited to send players to participate in a training camp over the Easter holidays. It was sponsored by 7-UP, and Billy Bingham, the then Northern Ireland manager, was one of the coaches. For three days, I got to play with and against McCarthy, Keane and O'Sullivan, in between doing drills under the baton of the Ulsterman who had led his country to the second round of the 1982 World Cup finals.

I learned very little from Bingham but I benefited hugely from the experience. How so? Well, having spent three days studying O'Sullivan, a boy then on the cusp of signing for Luton Town, I knew, for certain, that I would never be a professional footballer. The dream that started to fade the first time I witnessed his sorcery out in Whitechurch was now officially dead. It had to be. How could I ever possibly measure up to somebody of his gifts? I was as immature and narcissistic as any other teenager – but I wasn't totally blind to reality.

When I departed The Farm in UCC on the final day of the camp, I resolved to head back to school the following week with renewed determination to study. I knew now that, whatever else it held, my future definitely did not involve scouts from English clubs tracking my progress before making me a lucrative offer to sign on the dotted line.

A group of sixteen-year-old boys were leaning on their hurleys, standing in a circle around an irate man with a stick in his own hand. He was an All-Ireland senior medal-winner for Cork. He once brought the Liam MacCarthy cup to our school, waved it above his head and gave us a half-day from class as we roared our approval. A recent enough memory to ensure that we were hanging on his every word. Now and again, he punctuated his speechifying by bringing the hurley high above his head before then banging it off the grass for emphasis. The swish of it through the air impressed us more than the dull thud it made off the ground.

The purpose of this animated and increasingly violent soliloquy was to ensure we realised the gravity of just what was at stake in our next match. This was not just a county Under-16 A hurling final. This was St Finbarr's versus Midleton in 1987. The Hatfields versus the McCoys with participants wielding hurleys instead of rifles. Rangers versus Celtic without the unfortunate religious overtones and sectarian name-calling but with plenty of the same rancour. A peculiarly Gaelic version of Barcelona versus Real Madrid except the only diving would be for cover as timber was brandished and punches flew.

'No quarter given,' he said. 'No quarter asked.'

I had no idea what that phrase meant but it was a recurring theme in just about every pep talk we received back then, the gist of which was simple: once the whistle blows, anything goes.

'Any hand above head height is a legitimate target. Don't worry about hitting it. Not your fault if you break his fingers.'

We nodded like a squad of testosterone-fuelled teenage assassins being sent out to search and destroy. A few of us spit on the grass to show we were taking these instructions extra-seriously. Nobody even smirked.

'If a fella ends up on the ground near the ball and you accidentally hit his head as you swing on it, don't worry about it. We'll visit him in hospital.'

There was snorting now. From us, not him. Not the snorting of derisive laughter either. The snorting of earnest boys desperate to become men in this forthcoming battle, the kind of conflict where markers could be put down and reputations made. A boy who could do it in this kind of fixture would be identified as the type of character who might one day play senior in even more exacting arenas.

At that point in its illustrious history, St Finbarr's had twenty-four county senior hurling titles to its name, and a couple of club All-Irelands to boot. However, after seventy years in the wilderness, Midleton had emerged from the wilderness in East Cork and their breakthrough in 1983 came against a more fancied and storied Barrs' outfit. In Togher, that defeat smarted, especially since the upstarts hung around and won two more in the next four seasons. The nerve of these people. Like the dreaded bird after which they were nicknamed, the Mapgies were regarded as nothing but interlopers. Around our way, they were despised.

That we were mere juveniles, boy soldiers if you like, in this sporting war wasn't really a consideration. This war was fought on every front imaginable. No age group was exempt from the bitterness because, to us, this was new money versus old. The arrivistes from the country trying to overthrow the ancien régime from the city. And here was a man we looked up to, standing in front of us, reiterating again and again that we were charged with doing everything we could to hold on to the last vestiges of power. We weren't being asked to hurl. We were being asked to man the ramparts to repel the invading hordes.

We had trained for months for this encounter with the usurpers. Indeed, the build-up and run-in was so protracted that a couple of our starters got bored with the routine and began to skip sessions. Suddenly, the rumour went around that the selectors were rethinking the make-up of the settled fifteen that had won the city title back in the summer. Four nights before the final, they announced the team and the whispers proved true – I was chosen to play left-half-back.

This was a bit of a shock. I hadn't started or featured in any game in the entire campaign but here I was, promoted to the starting line-up. For the biggest clash of all. Why? Because, I hadn't missed a single session? Or I had been flying in training? I never did get an answer to that.

They gave us new blue socks that night and warned us to wash them once before Sunday so they were more comfortable in our boots. My mother was straight on the case.

On the bus ride to neutral Cobh that day, I felt great. No nerves. Just heady expectation. At last, my chance to shine on a big stage. As a boy, I'd played street leagues in Bishopstown and the Barrs but when the time came to pick one, I followed my brother to Bishopstown. At fourteen, I switched back to the Barrs. Easier said than done at a time when securing a transfer between GAA clubs in Cork involved a process akin to a resident of Moscow seeking permission from the politburo to leave the Soviet Union at the height of Communism.

I had to write a letter to the county board myself and I had to spend a season playing a year out of my age group. A bizarre Corkonian solution to a Corkonian problem. Once I got to play with my own peers again, I was trying to break into a team with tremendous talent and a settled line-up. No surprises then that I had spent the entire championship to that point wearing a tracksuit and mucking about with the rest of the vaguely embarrassed subs during half-time breaks. Finally, with Barra Naofa etched proudly in yellow across my chest, just like the one Jimmy Barry-Murphy wore, my hour had come.

'They have to be twice as good as us to beat us,' shouted one of the stalwarts in the dressing-room as we headed for the door. The snobbery. The arrogance. The confidence. It was wonderful. And we drank it in, running out onto the field with our chests puffed out. Full of it.

The first few minutes were faster than any of the training sessions in which I'd excelled. A couple of times the ball came into my possession. Once I grasped it in my hand and had the opportunity to clear downfield. I had time and I had space and I topped it straight to a white shirt lurking in the middle of the field. He lobbed it over the bar. The first nail in my coffin. Shortly after that, I ran on to a bouncing ball and went to swing on it first time. The sliotar went through the bas of my hurley like there was a hole in the centre of it. An air ball. The second nail.

The most basic skills I had been honing all my sporting life had suddenly deserted me when I needed them most. If I had swung at some Midleton boy's head, I would have probably ended up hitting one of my team-mates. Floundering like a boy out of his depth, I was drowning not waving. Everywhere I went, the ball seemed to have just left, often in the company of the man I was supposed to be marking. As I chased after him in vain it felt like I was running in treacle.

When the ball went out for a sideline in the Midleton half of the field, I noticed the play was taking a while to restart. I looked around to see if somebody was injured. Then I saw the referee looking rather pitfully in my direction and one of the Barrs' selectors with his right hand raised gesturing towards me. By his side, Eamon Fitzpatrick, the boy I'd replaced in the starting line-up, the usual left-half-back, was limbering up with the substitute's vital piece of paper in his hand.

I started to jog then I stopped. Unable to believe or to comprehend what was happening. I was being called ashore. Really? After twenty minutes! This was an era when tactical substitutions usually involved the ritualistic sacrifice of a woebegone corner-forward early in the second half who, through no fault of his own, had been starved of supply. I had never seen anybody taken off before half-time in any age group ever, unless he was hurt. I was not hurt. At least not physically. This was a first. Fresh ground. A new low.

Worse again, I didn't even have the wherewithal or the smarts to feign injury and limp towards the bench. Instead I started to run again, this time sprinting across the pitch as fast as I could. Desperate to get off the field where I had just embarrassed myself. Desperate to get out of sight of the crowd. My fellow subs, the ones I had spent the entire campaign hanging out with, offered a few words of condolences that I didn't really hear. I was oblivious. I pulled my Barrs' blue Cooper helmet down over my face as I tried to hide my shame.

At half-time I stayed rooted to the bench while the rest of the subs, those still harbouring hopes of seeing action, went through the perfunctory warm-up. I wanted to be anywhere else right then than at a county final in Cobh that I'd spent months preparing for, the kind of game I'd been years dreaming about. Never once, along the way, did I envisage the dream turning into a nightmare.

At one point in the second half, a scuffle broke out in the crowd behind the benches. A grown man who had represented Cork and Midleton with great distinction over the years, a hurling All-Star, was embroiled in a fist-fight with a boy I sat next to in primary school. Nobody seemed too perturbed at this tawdry spectacle of two spectators going at it. Tempers were bound to occasionally fray. It was the Barrs and Midleton. This is what a clash between these teams meant to people on both sides.

By then, the Barrs (their back line significantly more solid since the substitution I regarded as an infringement on my basic human rights) had got the upper hand. Not that I really cared who won anymore because that day I had already lost. I had lost something far more substantial. I had lost part of my love of the game forever.

I went through the motions of celebrating our victory at the final whistle. There were lads on that field, Gary Ring, Kieran Murphy, Ron and Finn Lehane, who I'd shared classrooms and schoolyards with since I was four years old. Plenty of other boys too that I'd hurled with and against when we cut our teeth in epic street league battles. I should have been happier for them as they sang their hearts out on the bus back to the clubhouse in Togher. I wasn't. I lip-synced to some of the songs because I didn't want to draw attention to myself. That was all I could do.

I put on my best smile for the subsequent meal and laughed loud at all the wisecracks but I didn't even taste the food. My cheeks hurt too much from faking the plastered-on grin people expected of a member of the triumphant squad. The whole club was en fête and I walked around pretending I was fine, trying to blend in, hoping nobody noticed the scarlet letter on my chest and recognised me as the guy who was taken off before half-time.

I was sisteen years old and life was mostly good. I'd discovered girls and was dating Jane, the younger sister of one of the club's stalwarts. I'd started to dabble in alcohol and was going to gigs in town on a regular basis. I'd just done an Inter Cert that was good enough for the school, in a move that was patronising yet conscientious, to inform my mother I should be thinking about going to UCC, a place nobody in our extended family had ever been. I even had an English teacher in Jed Kelly who, in a classic riff on *Dead Poets Society*, was encouraging me to write and write.

All positives, none of them mattered a damn that night. There was no possible consolation anywhere. I just wanted to be gone out of the Barrs' club. I wanted to go home to mourn my personal defeat in the midst of this historic victory. I wanted to go home to my bedroom to shut the door on the world and to try not to notice the Under-16 A hurling county winner's medal that was on my brother's shelf, the one he'd earned on the field of play three years earlier when he'd lasted the full hour, starring for Bishopstown.

This had been part of my excitement heading to Cobh that day. Here was the chance to play in front of a couple of thousand people, including friends and family, on a beautiful pitch, on a big day, just like my older brother. This represented sport at its most thrilling. Until it turned into sport at its most cruel yet instructive. Sometimes things just don't go your way. Somebody often has to be sacrificed for the greater good. And there are situations where feelings cannot be spared. Adults call it taking one for the team. Just another vital lesson the games taught me. A lesson for all of my life.

The moment I opened the door to my house that night, my mother was in the hallway to greet me, the rapid response unit, somebody who'd obviously been anticipating and probably dreading my arrival for hours. She took the gear bag with one hand and extended her other arm to draw me into her embrace.

'Don't worry about it, boy,' she whispered in my ear. 'It just wasn't your day. There'll be others.'

The story of a sporting life.

Sources

Dorgan, Val. *Christy Ring*, Ward River Press, Dublin, 1980.

Henchion, Richard. *The Land of the Finest Drop*. Dahadore Publications, Cork, 2003.

Horgan, Tim. *Cork's Hurling Story*, Anvil Books, Tralee, 1977.

www.kieranmccarthy.ie

O'Connell, Mick. *A Kerry Footballer*, Mercier Press, Cork, 1975.

Pritchard, DB. *Begin Chess*, Goodwin Publishing, Oldham, 1970.

SHOOT! magazine, 1977–88.

Tatarsky, Daniel. *Flick to Kick – An Illustrated History of Subbuteo*, Orion Books, London, 2004.